AMERICAN FORECASTER ALMANAC

1994

Business Edition

A Division of American Demographics, Inc.
127 West State Street, Ithaca, NY 14850
Telephone: 607-273-6343

Executive Editor: Diane Crispell
Associate Editor: Shannon Dortch
Associate Publisher: James Madden
Assistant Editor: Sarah Sirlin
Book Design and Composition: Rebecca Wilson

Hardcover: ISBN 0-936889-26-8
Paperback: ISBN 0-936889-25-X
ISSN 0897-8964

Cataloging In Publication Data
Long, Kim, 1949-
The American forecaster almanac, 1994 business edition

AMERICAN FORECASTER ALMANAC

1994

Business Edition

AMERICAN 📖
DEMOGRAPHICSBOOKS

K I M   L O N G

Contents

BUSINESS AND THE ECONOMY

HEALTH AND MEDICINE

SCIENCE AND COMPUTERS

THE CONSUMER

ENTERTAINMENT AND THE MEDIA

JOBS AND EDUCATION

FASHION

VACATIONS AND TRAVEL

SPORTS AND EXERCISE

Acknowledgements

The American Forecaster Almanac is created from information gathered from hundreds of sources. These include newspapers, periodicals, trade journals and newsletters, public information polls and surveys, industry surveys, statistical data from the U.S. government, and an occasional bit of inside information from private companies. For general resources relating to chapter topics, see the appendices at the end of this book.

Special assistance has been provided by the Denver Public Library, Kathleen Cain (Front Range Community College Library), Glenn King (statistical compendia staff, Bureau of the Census), Jim Williams (Norlin Library, University of Colorado), Pat Wagner and Leif Smith (Pattern Research), *The Bloomsbury Review*, Joyce Meskis (Tattered Cover), Robert McFarland, M.D., Randall Lockwood (Humane Society of the U.S.), Alice Price Knight, Ward Shaw (Colorado Association of Research Libraries), Richard Croog (Johnson Books), Chip Ransford (Nova Resources Group), Laurie Brock, Michael McNierney, Dennis Dube (Apple Development Lab), Greg Kirrish (Beatreme Foods), Steve Elliott (Facts is Facts), William Casey (Paris/Casey, Inc.), Bob Bonnell (Ground Zero Productions), Larry Sessions, Bert Paredes, Greg McNamee (Jungalitics), George Nash (PH Society), Steve Topping (Crown Publishers), Calorie Control Council, Food Technology Institute, William Schiemann (William Schiemann & Associates), National Association for the Cottage Industry, Cryopharm Corporation, Texas Internet Consulting, Generic Pharmaceutical Industry Association, American Society for Training and Development, Gary Yankton (Walking World), *Internet Business Report*, National Association of College Stores, Richard Mignogna (University of Denver), Mel Cozzens (Front Range Community College), and many more.

The American Forecaster does not accept money, gratuities, or anything of value in exchange for the publication of information about any business, product, or service. Businesses, products, and services are included for informative purposes only. No recommendation or endorsement is intended or implied. *The American Forecaster* philosophy is to provide information about changes in our society without criticism or favoritism. Editorial lapses in this policy can be expected in rare instances, not because of editorial bias, but from spending too much time looking at the human condition from close quarters.

INTRODUCTION

This edition of *The American Forecaster Almanac* marks the beginning of the second decade of publication. Like most endeavors in western civilization, ten years often marks a relatively significant milestone. Most likely because we are stuck with ten fingers, the decade is often used as a measure of progress.

Paul Harvey, the radio commentator whose career will reach the milestone of five decades of broadcasting in 1994, once stated, "Tomorrow has always been better than today." People are fascinated with the concept of the future, and particularly since the advent of the industrial revolution, they have linked "tomorrow" with the arrival of new and better lifestyles. This fascination, however, is rarely more than a passing curiosity for the general public.

For those in business, on the other hand, curiosity is increasingly replaced by a need to know. A new era of industry and global competition, a rising tide of information, and the arrival of new technologies have made awareness of the future a necessity for those in business enterprises.

Unfortunately, tools and knowledge with which to divine coming changes are not as accurate at those used in other professional activities. Objective analysis, observation, and historical perspective are about all that can be relied upon, along with a little common sense. Forecasting, however, often attracts more grandiose and subjective approaches. One current trend in forecasting is the reliance on wishful thinking and consumer attitudes to determine emerging changes. This approach, hereafter referred to as "babooning," often has appealing results, but stumbles in the face of reality. In the real world, large, significant, and entertaining changes rarely happen in a society, even over very long periods of time. The change experienced over the course of a few years, or even a decade, is more often boring and incremental than beguiling and massive.

As the world plods slowly forward, a preview of what to expect in the next year can be found in the following pages. New products such as insect-repellent tent fabric, freeze-dried blood, and neon turn signals for cars are covered, as well as changes for grocery stores, electronic mail, and gardening. Themes such as productivity, convenience, and interactivity are noted in numerous areas, including the corporate environment, retail sales, and entertainment. Discussion of ongoing trends, new developments, and implications with potential impact further ahead are also included.

If this collection proves disappointing to some, perhaps it is because it is missing speculation, fantasy, and nonverifiable information. For readers hankering for something with less substance and more pizzazz, look under "babooning" in the Yellow Pages.

—the author

"Quod enim mavult homo verum esse,
id potius credit." *—Francis Bacon*

(For what a man would like to be true,
that he more readily believes.)

U.S. VITAL STATISTICS FOR 1994

	1994	1984
Population	260 million	236 million
Median age	35 years	31.3 years
Births	4.0 million	3.7 million
Birth rate	67/1000 women	65.4/1000 women
Abortions	1.3 million	1.6 million
Infant mortality rate	9/1000 births	10.8/1000 births
Marriages	2.0 million	2.5 million
Divorces	1.0 million	1.2 million
Number of households	97 million	85 million
Average household size	2.6 persons	2.71 persons
Deaths	2.2 million	2.0 million
Life expectancy at birth, male	73 years	71 years
Life expectancy at birth, female	80 years	78 years
Never-married male adults (percent of population)	27 percent	25.5 percent
Never-married female adults (percent of population)	20 percent	18.4 percent
New housing starts	1.2 million	1.7 million
Per capita income	$24,700	$13,120
Population below poverty level	40.1 million	33.7 million
Median price of new one-family house	$120,000	$79,900
Americans without health insurance (percent of population)	14 percent	15 percent
Total health expenditures	$975 billion	$390 billion
Number of hospital beds	1.0 million	1.3 million
Outpatient visits	450 million	277 million

U.S. VITAL STATISTICS FOR 1994

	1994	1984
Patent applications	185,000	121,000
Pieces of mail handled	160 billion	132 billion
Sporting-goods sales	$50 billion	$26 billion
Exercise-equipment sales	$2.5 billion	$1.1 billion
Alcohol consumption	38 gallons/person	41 gallons/person
Charitable contributions	$145 billion	$70 billion
Regular church-goers (percent of population)	38 percent	41 percent
Federal and state prisoners	900,000	445,399
Opera attendance	25 million	13 million
Major-league-baseball attendance	60 million	45 million
Horse-racing attendance	57 million	74 million
Number of Boy Scouts	5.6 million	4.8 million
Number of Girl Scouts	3.7 million	2.9 million
Number of trips outside the U.S.	49 million	34 million
Number of foreign visitors to U.S.	49 million	27 million
Compact-disc production—music	500 million	6 million
Record production (LPs)	1 million	205 million
Prerecorded tapes	200 million	332 million
Cellular-phone subscribers	20 million	92,000
Households with cable TV (percent of households)	60 percent	41 percent
Households with VCRs (percent of households with a TV)	75 percent	11 percent
Advertising expenditures	$140 billion	$88 billion

U.S. VITAL STATISTICS FOR 1994

	1994	1984
Use of recovered paper	32 million tons	17 million tons
Books: average annual expenditures per consumer	$190	$132
Number of franchised stores	600,000	444,000
Fish consumption	14 pounds/person	14 pounds/person
Chicken consumption	64 pounds/person	56 pounds/person
Fresh-vegetable consumption	115 pounds/person	81 pounds/person
Frozen-vegetable consumption	21 pounds/person	12 pounds/person
Mozzarella-cheese consumption	9 pounds/person	4 pounds/person
Shoplifting offenses	1.4 million	891,000
Homicides	22,300	19,800
Household burglaries	4.8 million	3.0 million
AIDS cases reported	46,000	4,445
AIDS deaths	18,000	3,266
Cancer deaths	548,000	454,566
Visits to national parks	60 million	50 million
Personal-computer shipments	9.5 million	8 million
Modem shipments	3.5 million	960,000

1984 statistics from The Statistical Abstract of the United States 1987 *and other editions, plus* Agricultural Statistics 1992, USDA.

Note: Additional agricultural statistics may be found in "Farm Forecasts," page 36.
Additional educational statistics may be found in "School Statistics," page 205.

ANNIVERSARIES IN 1994

500TH ANNIVERSARIES — EVENTS OF 1494

Jamaica was discovered by Christopher Columbus during his second voyage to the new world.

Spain and Portugal compromised their explorations with the Treaty of Tordesillas, ceding newly discovered lands to each country based on a north-south line about 1,000 miles to the west of the Azores.

200TH ANNIVERSARIES — EVENTS OF 1794

The Intelligencer Journal (Lancaster, Pennsylvania) and the *Rutland Herald* (Rutland, Vermont) began publishing.

Bowdoin College (Brunswick, Maine) and the University of Tennessee (Knoxville) were founded.

Benjamin Franklin published his autobiography.

The maximum-minimum thermometer was invented.

March 14   Eli Whitney received a patent for his invention of the cotton gin.

March 27   The U.S. Navy was created by legislation signed by President Washington.

June 10   The Bethel African Methodist Church was established by Richard Allen (Philadelphia, Pennsylvania).

August 7   President Washington ordered militia to respond to a citizen uprising in western Pennsylvania. This unrest, known as the Whiskey Rebellion, was precipitated by a new federal excise tax on whiskey.

100TH ANNIVERSARIES — EVENTS OF 1894

New York City passed the first dog-licensing law in the U.S.

The U.S. Golf Association was founded.

Ralston Purina was founded (St. Louis, Missouri).

Lowell Observatory opened.

Billboard magazine and the *Daily Racing Form* were first published.

Plasterboard was invented.

The board game Parcheesi was introduced.

The first running shoe was invented.

The Kellogg brothers invented the first flaked breakfast cereal (Battle Creek, Michigan).

The first children's division in a public library opened (Denver, Colorado).

August 8   The Republic of Hawaii was officially recognized by the U.S. government following an abortive revolution led by Queen Liliuokalani the preceding year.

50TH ANNIVERSARIES — EVENTS OF 1944

The first eye bank opened (New York City).

Aaron Copland wrote *Appalachian Spring.*

Seventeen magazine began publishing.

Paul Harvey began broadcasting the news.

Tetracycline was discovered.

General Electric introduced "bouncing putty," later renamed Silly Putty.

January 22   U.S. armed forces landed at Anzio, Italy.

June 5   Allied armed forces entered Rome.

June 6   The Normandy landings began in France.

July 6   A circus fire at the Ringling Brothers and Barnum and Bailey Circus killed 167 people (Hartford, Connecticut).

July 20   U.S. forces landed on Guam.

September 7   The first V-2 rocket was launched toward London by German forces.

September 8   The first recorded impact of a V-2 killed two people.

October 20   U.S. forces landed on Leyte.

December 16   German forces initiated the Battle of the Bulge.

December 24   Band leader Glenn Miller died in a plane crash in Europe.

25TH ANNIVERSARIES — EVENTS OF 1969

All-male Princeton University began admitting women for the first time in its history.

The scanning electron microscope was perfected.

DHL Worldwide Express, Wendy's Hamburgers, Celestial Seasonings, Storage Technology Corporation, Friends of the Earth, and the National Taxpayers Union were founded.

Followers of Charles Manson went on a murder spree in California, the trial of the Chicago Eight began, Native-American activists invaded Alcatraz Island, and the first drawing was held for the draft lottery.

January 20   Richard Nixon was inaugurated as the 37th president of the United States.

April 4   The first artificial heart was implanted in a human (Houston, Texas).

July 20   The first human set foot on the moon.

August 15   The Woodstock Music and Art Fair began (Bethel, New York).

BIRTHDAYS IN 1994

60 YEARS OLD IN 1994
(born in 1934)

January 16	Marilyn Horne
January 17	Shari Lewis
January 30	Tammy Grimes
February 9	John Ziegler
February 13	George Segal
February 14	Florence Henderson
February 17	Alan Bates
February 27	Ralph Nader
March 11	Sam Donaldson
March 25	Gloria Steinem
March 26	Alan Arkin
March 31	Shirley Jones
April 10	David Halberstam
May 19	Jim Lehrer
May 22	Peter Nero
June 1	Pat Boone
June 5	Bill Moyers
June 19	Gena Rowlands
June 20	Martin Landau
June 30	Harry Blackstone, Jr.

July 1   Jamie Farr
July 1   Sidney Pollack
July 12   Van Cliburn
July 17   Donald Sutherland
August 22   Norman Schwarzkopf
August 23   Barbara Eden
September 5   Carol Lawrence
September 10   Charles Kuralt
September 20   Sophia Loren
September 27   Wilford Brimley
September 27   Greg Morris
September 28   Brigitte Bardot
November 9   Carl Sagan
November 19   Larry King
December 5   Joan Didion
December 9   Junior Wells

50 YEARS OLD IN 1994
(born in 1944)

January 6   Bonnie Franklin
January 16   Ronnie Milsap
January 23   Rutger Hauer
January 31   Sharon Pratt Dixon
January 31   Jessica Walter
February 5   Al Kooper
February 9   Alice Walker
February 13   Stockard Channing
February 23   Johnny Winter
March 1   Roger Daltrey
March 6   Kiri Te Kanawa
March 15   Sly Stone
March 17   John Sebastian
March 26   Diana Ross
March 28   Ken Howard
April 3   Tony Orlando
April 30   Jill Clayburgh
May 4   William Bennett

May 14	George Lucas
May 20	Joe Cocker
May 25	Frank Oz
May 27	Christopher Dodd
June 4	Michelle Phillips
June 8	Boz Scaggs
June 24	Jeff Beck
June 29	Gary Busey
July 31	Geraldine Chaplin
August 8	Peter Weir
August 9	Sam Elliott
September 1	Archie Bell
September 6	Swoosie Kurtz
September 12	Barry White
September 13	Jacqueline Bisset
September 14	Joey Heatherton
September 25	Michael Douglas
October 4	Pattie LaBelle
October 31	Kinky Friedman
November 11	Jesse Colin Young
November 12	Al Michaels
November 17	Danny DeVito
December 11	Brenda Lee
December 19	Tim Reid

40 YEARS OLD IN 1994
(born in 1954)

January 22	Chris Lemmon
January 29	Oprah Winfrey
February 18	John Travolta
March 17	Leslie-Ann Down
March 28	Reba McEntire
April 8	John Schneider
April 9	Dennis Quaid
May 8	David Keith
June 15	Jim Belushi
June 19	Kathleen Turner
July 6	Allyce Beasley

July 30	Ken Olin
August 18	Patrick Swayze
August 25	Elvis Costello
September 7	Corbin Bernsen
September 12	Peter Scolari
November 3	Adam Ant
November 8	Rickie Lee Jones
December 11	Jermaine Jackson
December 28	Denzel Washington

30 YEARS OLD IN 1994
(born in 1964)

January 7	Nicolas Cage
February 18	Matt Dillon
March 10	Jasmine Guy
May 8	Melissa Gilbert-Brinkman
November 27	Robin Givens

BUSINESS AND THE ECONOMY

BUSINESS AND THE ECONOMY

The expected economic rebound from the recent recession did not materialize in 1993 and may also avoid an appearance in 1994. The next year may, in fact, stimulate demand for a new term to describe the ongoing economic conditions. This slow, moderate growth might best be described as a "procession," generally heading in a positive direction but not in any hurry to get there.

From multinational corporations to home-based sole proprietorships, businesses will be slimming down and shaping up to be success-ful in a tough economic climate. Technology will play no small part in business trends in 1994, as companies make the most of com-puters and improved telecommunications to be more efficient.

THE ECONOMY IN 1994

Economic forecasts generated by *The American Forecaster Almanac* are based on a wide range of predictions generated by economics and industry analysts. Generally speaking, extreme positions are discounted, and averages are used. As the Roman poet Ovid once stated, *"Medio tutissimus ibis"* — "A middle course is the safest for you to take."

GROSS NATIONAL PRODUCT 3 percent growth

FEDERAL DEFICIT $300 billion

BALANCE OF TRADE
Merchandise: -$100 billion
Services: $70 billion

INFLATION RATE (Consumer Price Index): 3.5 percent

INTEREST RATES
Prime rate: 6.0 percent (lowest)
General direction: up
T-bills (3 month): 4.0 percent

PERSONAL SAVINGS 7 percent of disposable income

AVERAGE CORPORATE PROFIT
10 percent increase (after taxes)

STOCK MARKET
Dow Jones Average: 3900 (high point for the year)

CRUDE OIL $20 per barrel (year-end average)

GASOLINE $1.30 per gallon (U.S. average)

PRECIOUS METALS
Gold: $350 per ounce
Silver: $5 per ounce

UNEMPLOYMENT 6.5 percent

MORTGAGE RATES 8.0 percent (average high fixed rate)

HOUSING
New housing starts: 1.2 million
Median price of a new house: $137,000

The Future of Business

Under the buzzword "reengineering," a widespread movement is pushing reform on businesses from the inside out. Service and manufacturing industries alike are beginning to change as a means of survival, if not expansion, in today's ever-evolving economic climate. Reengineering utilizes new corporate structures—management, lines of communication, work groups, planning, etc.—to improve productivity, quality, and flexibility.

Reengineering involves both theoretical and structural changes within business. Companies attack productivity and service problems by analyzing how their internal systems of management and production work, then institute radical changes to permit more efficient use of their resources. The process is likely to involve new tools such as computer hardware and software, but it also focuses on the basic nature of how employees interact, innovate, and function in groups.

"The systems in large companies are like grandma's attic," says industrial psychologist Bill Casey, a specialist in corporate organizational design. "Piece after piece has been added without regard for overall organization until the place is a mess." Reengineering as applied to this metaphor would mean reorganizing the entire attic and "questioning what you want to keep, what you want to toss, and what you want to start collecting," Casey says.

Reengineering is a major change involving departments, all levels of management, and other aspects of a business' structure and internal processes. Smaller changes might improve efficiency in parts of a company, but reengineering is necessary for a complete overhaul. An example of a limited fix, process improvement involves "going into the attic, sorting and labeling a box of old photographs, and throwing out unwanted duplicates," says Casey, who works with businesses under-going change. "This doesn't improve the attic overall, but at least now you can find and file photos efficiently."

Like many effective changes in business, reengineering often has as much to do with simple, practical answers as with complex, sophisti-cated change. While undergoing this process, businesses study their methods of operation, which are as likely to be missing small compo-nents as requiring complete overhauls. Reengineering borrows solutions from the past, combines multiple activities, and creates new applica-tions to address problems.

Here are some aspects of reengineering (many are themselves be-coming management buzzwords):

■ **Flexibility** This is one of the most important aspects of reengi-neering and one at which U.S. businesses excel. Flexibility involves more than the ability to turn out new products. In the service industries, it is a cultural characteristic that allows workers to adapt to new conditions quickly. The North American culture is traditionally more open to new ideas and changing environments than other countries because of the diverse background of the population. Unlike more rigid worker cultures, employees in the U.S. are more likely to have worked in more than one type of job or industry, have more positive expectations about their capabilities, and rely less on family work history in finding careers.

■ **Total quality management** Already a widespread program used for internal reforms in private businesses and government entities, TQM has been criticized for its improper use by organizations, but its basic tenets are in use in the reengineering movement. They include empow-erment of workers, improved communications between departments and management levels, defining of goals, incentives for worker improve-ment, and commitment to improving the quality of products or ser-vices. TQM is usually implemented as a change in process within a com-pany, rather than a change in structure, a hallmark of reengineering.

■ **Computerization** Computer applications that are used in re-engineering include image processing (turning documents, photographs, or other graphics into digital forms for storage, manipulation, or tele-communications), telecommunications, expert systems (software pro-grams that can perform some "intelligent" functions such as searching, filing, or analyzing data), groupware (software designed to permit efficient sharing of resources and computer-based work by more than one person), and voice processing (using computer hardware and software to translate and interpret spoken words into digital messages, and vice versa). New technologies that will aid reengineering include computerized inventory systems with direct ordering links to customers, "paperless" document management systems that decrease inefficient handling of forms, "smart" telephones that reduce the need for operator assistance, high-speed data networks that increase the speed of delivery of information, desktop design centers for rapid development of new products, and automated electronic billing and banking.

■ **Service** This is perhaps the hottest buzzword in reengineering. The quest to improve service is likely to grow more intense in coming years as businesses newly define who their customers are and improve relationships with them.

■ **Downsizing** Ideally, downsizing turns fewer personnel into a more productive work force. Downsizing in service industries can be used to restructure management and reduce traditional bureaucratic inefficiencies.

■ **Ongoing education** Workers and even business owners are no longer able to rely on a single education period, such as college, to prepare them for the working world. College educations will increasingly include on-the-job training, such as internships, and businesses will provide more financial incentives for workers' college educations while keeping them on the job. Management is part of this new perpetual education cycle, with part-time programs adding appropriate new skills through seminars, business-school extensions, and on-site advanced training. The ongoing education of managers and executives may also include what is known as action learning—hands-on practice in solving problems. (See also "Action-Learning Allure," page 199.)

A small cloud of dissatisfaction, however, is already hovering over the reengineering movement. Precipitated by several years of misuse of related programs, such as those listed above, many companies are convinced that reengineering does not work. In a recent survey of company executives conducted by the management consulting firm William Schiemann & Associates, less than half of the respondents reported meeting objectives for change with programs designed to do just that.

The survey did find that change was more likely to be accomplished when executives understood and agreed upon the programs being utilized and were able to communicate the process and effects to employees. This included imparting a clear understanding of the consequences of new processes and new organizational structures. Change was also facilitated when management and employees were willing to tackle the difficult problem of changing the corporate culture.

Schiemann, president of William Schiemann & Associates, and other business analysts believe that change—especially significant change—must occur from the top down. Simply delegating the latest trendy reorganization program to managers for implementation will not result in effective change.

While reengineering failures are easy to find, success stories show that the individual programs that are used for reengineering are not always the cause of the failure. Sometimes the scope and complexity involved in implementing a major program may be overwhelming for a company. The small commonplace changes businesses make, such as initiating flextime or evaluating customer service, are relatively simple compared with the massive, cross-functional, and usually disruptive change involved in reengineering. At the same time, the rewards of reengineering are clear. Reengineering helps companies develop efficient and flexible staffs. And those companies are the ones most likely to survive the impact of international competition, new technology, changing employee demographics, and chaotic political climates, all of which are facts of business life in the 1990s.

RESOURCES:

William Schiemann & Associates
Somerville, NJ
(908) 231-1900
(management consulting service specializing in organizational assessment and change management)

Paris/Casey, Inc.
Portland, OR
(503) 287-7000
(management consultants specializing in organizational design)

Michael Anderson, Johnson Smith, Fromkin McCullough
Toronto, Ontario
(416) 365-1865
(management consulting)

American Productivity and Quality Center
Houston, TX
(713) 681-4020
(national organization working with businesses and other organizations to improve productivity, quality, and quality of work life)

Journal of Systems Management
published by Association for
Systems Management
Cleveland, OH
(216) 243-6900

Industrial Engineering
published by Institute of
Industrial Engineers
Norcross, GA
(404) 449-0460

Association of Productivity
Specialists
New York, NY
(212) 286-0943
(industry association of
professionals involved with
productivity)

Other Business Trends

NEW OFFICE POSITIONS Some companies are developing new employee positions as a result of demand, technology, and increasing worker productivity. Among the new jobs are:

- **ombudsmen,** problem-solvers for employee-management disputes.

- **environmental directors,** managers who plan and oversee energy usage, pollution control, and recycling.

- **office moms,** all-purpose support employees who provide emergency assistance, errand-running, food delivery, party catering, and special-events planning.

- **managers of technology,** management specialists trained in the use, acquisition, or manufacture of technology, especially computers. (See also "Managing Technology," page 203.)

BUSINESS COACHES Anecdotal reports indicate the existence of a new brand of consultants specializing in various aspects of business start-ups, management, and growth. Not unlike mentors, these business coaches are more likely to concentrate on the business than the individual. Especially for small businesses, these coaches use personal experience to help with start-ups and expansions.

GROWTH CEILING Many small businesses in this decade may hit a growth ceiling of 49 employees. Several new federal laws—the Americans with Disabilities Act and the Family and Medical Leave Act—mandate compliance only for companies of 50 or more employees, which is an incentive for businesses to cap employment at 49. Some small companies have already downsized to keep below this limit, and surveys indicate other businesses plan to follow suit. Even though the number of employees in a company will be reduced, the overall effect may be improved productivity and reductions in overhead. As companies learn to make do with fewer workers, they will be forced to find ways to be more efficient producers, or hire part-time or temporary workers at lower wages than are paid to full-time employees.

RESOURCES:

National Federation of Independent
Business
Washington, DC
(202) 554-9000
(industry association of independent
businesses and professionals)

BANK CHANGES More banks are expected to dispense with returning canceled checks to customers in favor of statements with reproduced images of the checks. "Image statements," already in use by some major banks and credit-card companies, such as American Express, condense required material to much less space. Other bank trends include increased use of ATM machines that are not part of a customer's bank, "talking" ATM machines that use voice processing to replace personal identification numbers (PIN numbers) with voice recognition, voice-controlled banking by telephone, and credit authorization by telephone in as little as six seconds.

RESOURCES:

InterVoice
Dallas, TX
(214) 497-8771
(voice identification systems
for banking)

NCR
Dayton, OH
(513) 445-5000
(voice identification ATMs)

IBM Document and Check Imaging
Charlotte, NC
(704) 594-8008
(proof-of-deposit imaging system)

AT&T InterSpan Transaction
Access Service
Morristown, NJ
(800) 247-1212
(document imaging)

Electronic Funds Transfer
Association
Herndon, VA
(703) 435-9800
(industry association of banks and
financial institutions)

National Association for Check
Safekeeping
Herndon, VA
(703) 742-9190
(industry association involved with
banking transactions; part of
National Automated Clearing
House)

*Products, Marketing and Technology:
Banking Issues and Innovations*
published by Bank Administration
Institute, Chicago, IL
(312) 553-4600

ALTERNATIVE ADVANCEMENTS With fewer management levels and positions in many companies, there are fewer conventional advancement opportunities for management personnel. In order to retain and reward valued workers, some of today's leaner companies are responding by developing new nonmanagerial career paths. Positions such as senior manager, team leader, department head, and partner are being replaced with positions such as internal consultant, internal analyst, director, vice chairman, and individual contributor.

Advantages for businesses include increased employee loyalty and satisfaction and more fulfilling work for senior employees not interested in traditional management activities. Disadvantages include discrepancies in pay and workloads between workers in the new positions and traditional manager positions. Negative reports also indicate workers in these new positions can lack accountability.

RESOURCES:

American Management Association
New York, NY
(212) 586-8100
(industry association of managers
in business, government,
noncommercial organizations,
administrators, and university
teachers of management)

FOREIGN SEWN Most recent major bases for foreign production of American clothes have been in Asia, with China on the ascent. But potential political changes in the trading status between the U.S. and China, as well as rising costs in that country and other Asian centers, have pushed manufacturers to find other places for skilled labor, low costs, and reliable quality, such as El Salvador, Guatemala, Honduras, Mexico, Lesotho, Kenya, Malawi, Dubai, and Israel. Anticipation is also building for potentially strong manufacturing markets in Bulgaria, Hungary, Russia, and other former East Bloc countries, although questions remain about consistent and reliable political conditions, long-term affordable labor costs, and production quality.

RESOURCES:

American Apparel Manufacturers
Association
Arlington, VA
(703) 524-1864
(industry association of apparel
makers)

Home Work Impediments

Although the trend of more people working at home is not likely to decline in the rest of the decade, it is unclear how much it may grow. This group of workers is estimated at 15 to 30 million, but most sources agree that the size is now increasing.

In spite of its appeal, working at home is not for everyone. Some studies indicate that a sizable proportion of office workers—15 to 75 percent—would resist working at home if given the opportunity. A lack of appropriate work space and the presence of distractions and family members can make offices a necessary escape for many. At the same time, business consultants report an increasing number of workers want the best of both environments: a comfortable work space at home in which to do focused tasks and concentrate on productivity, and a convivial environment in a company office where they can communicate face-to-face with peers and be part of a traditional office "family."

Additional difficulties for independent workers have been created recently by new IRS rules on deducting home-office expenses. Beginning in 1994, the new guidelines eliminate previously valid deductions for many people employed in home-based businesses. This change will have an immediate negative effect on the financial ability of many home-based enterprises to survive.

Like most changes in government standards, however, the initial shock may be worse than the long-term effect of the change. The new IRS rules will certainly harm many home businesses and may discourage some people from starting up new home-based businesses. Within a few years, however, natural entrepreneurial forces will cause the number of home businesses to rebound.

Many home-based firms will adapt to the new rules by becoming incorporated. Incorporation creates a legal entity that can shield its principals from some business liabilities. In a residence, it can help home-based businesses segregate business costs from family expenditures. A new industry may emerge to help home-based businesses make the switch to incorporation at low cost and with a minimum of hassle. Consultants, seminars, computer programs, videotapes and audiotapes, books, do-it-yourself kits, and other products and services can be expected.

Simply incorporating may not be enough for most home businesses. They will also have to distinguish their business and home addresses. This could fuel a new boom in use for shared office spaces, "office suites" where phones, copiers, and receptionists are shared by renters. Office suite entrepreneurs may use the new tax rules for home firms as a marketing plug for their services and develop new sites that are more convenient to former home businesses. Competition may also push prices down, drawing even more home firms to shared office space.

For entrepreneurs who want to stay in homes, remodeling activity may pick up as attempts are made to create more physically separate facilities for firms. Office space may be moved into garages, barns, and outbuildings, and in neighborhoods where home businesses are proliferating, neighbors may collaborate to create shared office space.

At the other extreme, there may be an increase in nonregistered businesses and "moonlighting" enterprises. This may result in a decrease rather than increase in federal tax revenue. Because of widespread enthusiasm for home businesses, however, grassroots pressure and political rhetoric may prompt a return to more liberal tax deductions for home-based businesses. If such a reversal does occur, it is most likely to be within the next three to five years.

RESOURCES:

National Association for the
Cottage Industry
Chicago, IL
(312) 472-8116
(industry association of home-based
businesses)

National Association of Home Based
Businesses
Owings Mills, MD
(410) 363-3698
(industry association of home-based
businesses)

*The Kern Report: Trends and Issues
in Home-Based Business and
Telecommuting*
published by National Association
for the Cottage Industry
Chicago, IL
(312) 472-8116

E-Mail
Madness

The advent of the electronic-mail era has created a sense of empower-
ment for many businesses and professionals. The attraction of e-mail is
its simplified and automated routing of written correspondence. However, the popularity of this technology has led to e-mail overload.
E-mail users increased from about 12 million in 1990 to more than 20
million in 1992. At this volume, an increasing number of companies
and individuals are having difficulty reading and replying to their
e-mail correspondence.

Adding to the ever-flowing stream of electronic messages are those
associated with the Internet. The Internet is a national system of computer networks with links throughout the world, allowing rapid interchange of digital information. Through the Internet, any user can send
electronic mail to any other user. According to at least one estimate (no
accurate figures or estimates are available), as of April 1993, there were
1.5 million "hosts" on the Internet. Each of these hosts represents either a computer or a computer connection to other computers. Some
large companies have thousands or tens of thousands of computers
linked through their own internal networks. Internet users are found
at government, military, research, and academic sites.

Just as with the overuse of facsimile machines, e-mail has generated junk messages, advertising, notices that once would have been
pinned to bulletin boards, duplicated memos and letters, and lengthy
missives from downloaded files. That has left many office workers with
a crippling overload of electronic information. But e-mail as it is now is
already being transformed into a new technology: telephone-based voice-
mail and computer-based e-mail will be combined, producing desktop
voice mail.

The new technology will allow single-screen access to both e-mail messages and electronically translated voice-mail messages, now delivered via telephone. These voice-generated messages could be stored in digital files, added to word-processed documents, and sent through local and wide-area networks to other workers. In essence, the desktop voice-mail technology could eliminate the need for most dictation or retyping services.

Desktop voice-mail is being developed by several large computer companies, including IBM and Digital. Both call the technology Computer Telephone Integration (CTI). Desktop voice-mail should be on the market in two to four years. Meanwhile, currently available voice-processing products include text-to-speech conversion programs and an increasing number of products for applications such as medical information entry.

Finally, the adoption of an industry standard for desktop voice-mail is pending. It is under development by both the Voice Mail User Interface Forum and the Audio Messaging Interexchange Specification (AMIS).

Other E-mail Trends

E-MAIL SECRETARIES Some executives who are now humanized by their e-mail connectiveness will resurrect the traditional role of secretaries. These computer-based workers will screen incoming e-mail to reduce the workload of their bosses. Software programs are already being created to perform this function, but human training and skills are likely to win out over software where expense is less important than prestige. The e-mail secretary may be either male or female and may work from a remote location. His or her presence would only be required on the computer screen. Many of today's executives have reached their present levels without becoming computer literate. They continue to use the precursor to the e-mail secretary—the assistant who takes dictated letters and memos and creates hard-copy letters on word processors or e-mail with the boss's byline. These more traditional executive secretaries are often trusted with safe combinations and keys to private offices, and are permitted to file and retrieve documents from their bosses' desks and filing cabinets. E-mail secretaries will have similar responsibilities, but instead of keys, they will use passwords and codes to allow them to perform their digital duties.

E-MAIL BULLETIN BOARDS Instead of routing all e-mail messages to individuals, some companies are resurrecting an electronic version of an old business standard—the office bulletin board. Memos and announcements that are now broadcast to all individuals on an e-mail network are routed instead to a central digital posting point. Just as the traditional office bulletin board provided a platform for general announcements, regulations, and changes in company policies with the e-mail bulletin board, individuals can reduce clutter on their private e-mail accounts.

E-MAIL BUNDLING E-mail is becoming a common feature of many software programs. Computer operating systems, including those from Apple Computer and Microsoft, soon will include e-mail links, including both System 7 (Macintosh) and Windows (Microsoft).

RESOURCES:

Active Voice Corporation
Seattle, WA
(206) 441-4700
(voice processing systems)

Applied Voice Technology, Inc.
Kirkland, WA
(206) 820-6000
(voice processing systems)

Centigram Communications
Corporation
San Jose, CA
(408) 944-0250
(audio information processing
systems)

VMX, Inc.
San Jose, CA
(408) 441-1166
(integrated voice processing
systems)

Advantis
(800) 284-5849
Schaumburg, IL
(IBM/Sears joint venture for e-mail
services)

Digital Equipment Corporation
Electronic Mail and EDI Systems
Nashua, NH
(508) 493-5111
(e-mail services)

Dataquest, Inc.
San Jose, CA
(408) 437-8000
(market research)

Electronic Mail Association
Arlington, VA
(703) 524-5550
(industry association for businesses
involved with e-mail)

Meeting the Future

From economic changes to structural changes within corporations, meeting planners, convention officials, and trade associations are living with an industry at the beginning of a transition period.

One of the greatest factors affecting meetings is lack of facilities expansive enough to accommodate the largest trade-association conventions. Insufficient hotel space, too few meeting rooms, and inadequate exhibition space are all crimping growth of the biggest events. Because the largest sites have little flexibility, the conflict will most likely mean more rules restricting exhibitors, exhibit size, and presentation assignments. The ever-changing and increasingly competitive business climate means more information than ever. And information gathering is the primary reason to hold meetings.

Other Convention and Meeting Trends

FOREIGN INTERCHANGE A greater number of foreigners will be attending U.S. meetings, which means meeting planners will need to provide translation services and be more aware of different customs, diets, and etiquette. On the other hand, an increasing global use of English for business will decrease the number of visitors with no grasp of the local language. That trend actually may help boost foreign participation at U.S. meetings.

The united European market and the pending North American Free Trade Agreement (NAFTA) may create more potential for meetings traditionally held in the U.S. to move to other countries. Smaller meetings may be more likely to have the flexibility to go abroad, but even the largest trade shows may be lured across the border.

At least in this decade, Toronto is the only city close enough to the U.S. with major transportation connections and facilities large enough to handle a large trade show. Since construction and labor costs are lower in Canada and Mexico than in the U.S., cities in those countries may quickly develop large centers for trade shows. The advantage for American businesses will be lower costs for space, new and exotic locales, and lower lodging and dining expenses.

TRAVEL COST CONTAINMENT Multiple industry-specific trade shows may be a dying breed, as rising travel costs and leaner operating budgets restrict the number of shows employees can attend. The companies that send personnel to shows are likely to exercise tighter control over meeting participation and be more selective about which meetings to attend. The effect on the meeting industry is likely to be heightened competition, increased marketing and advertising, and participant incentives to bolster attendance. Trade shows whose programs are similar to other shows may fold or merge with others. Despite rising travel costs, however, meeting attendees will benefit from improved presentations, careful organization, more substantive content, and greater consistency in seminar and speaking quality.

SHRINK FACTOR While competitive and other pressures may bring an end to smaller and lesser-known industry meetings, the importance and established expectations from the largest trade shows and major professional meetings are here to stay. However, medium and small shows will respond to attendees' time and money constraints by sponsoring shorter shows in more convenient locations. Planners will favor hotels and conference centers close to airports or major urban centers.

EXPERT ADVICE Both internal and independent meeting consultants will become more widely used by companies that are limiting travel, trying to make the most efficient use of meeting time, and eliminating attendance at duplicate trade shows. These consultants will provide guidance on controlling their clients' travel costs.

TARGETING HOME BUSINESSES Meeting formats, schedules, and locations are evolving to meet the needs of home-based businesses. Although these workers are linked to the world through e-mail, facsimile transmissions, and telephone, they still need verbal discussions and group interchange to make many of their most important business decisions. Especially for workers whose home-based businesses are far from centers of commerce, meetings will gain significance as places to network, make job contacts, keep tabs on developments in their fields, and simply enjoy contact with others. The meeting industry will be doing more direct marketing to attract home-based workers to conferences, provide more personal services, and make meetings more productive.

MEETING TECHNOLOGY Companies' desires to control meeting costs have helped boost development of at least one technology that can reduce the need for face-to-face meetings. Groupware is computer networking software with which workers share ideas and information among disparate computer work stations. In meetings, groupware allows simultaneous entry of ideas, comments, and information by meeting participants, with the resulting flow of information displayed on a large screen. The advantage of groupware for this use is that it is inherently more democratic than most meetings. Individuals participate without being shut out of a discussion because of lack of conversation skills or other personal limitations. Variations of groupware are designed for simple voting or participant feedback during presentations. (See also "Fast Track for Video Conferencing," page 32.)

RESOURCES:

International Association for
Exposition Management
Indianapolis, IN
(317) 871-7272
(industry association for managers, suppliers, and services involved with trade shows and expositions)

Meeting Planners International
Dallas, TX
(214) 712-7702
(industry association for meeting planners, suppliers, and consultants)

International Association of
Conference Centers
St. Louis, MO
(314) 993-8575
(industry association of personnel involved with executive, resort, and other conference centers)

Fast Track for Video Conferencing

Thanks to video conferencing technology, "distance meetings"—those that link participants in far-flung locations—are becoming more common. Some new technology and products are emerging, but lower prices for video-conferencing equipment are what is really driving increased use. Annual sales of video-conferencing equipment have doubled over the past three years. Equipment sales totaled $330 million in 1992, according to the Yankee Group, and are expected to reach $600 million in 1994.

Stand-alone systems will account for much of this growth, but the near future may see personal-computer-based video-conferencing equipment. New systems due out shortly include the product of a joint venture between PictureTel Corporation and Lotus Development, a "picture-in-picture" image that will allow workers at different locations to see each other or other images while working within other software applications, such as spreadsheets or word processing. VideoTelecom Corporation is getting in on the act also with Deskmax, a system designed to run in Microsoft's Windows environment. It is expected to be available in late 1993 or 1994 and sell for about $15,000.

PC-based video-conferencing hardware and software now run on 486-generation PCs. But with the arrival of new PCs powered by Intel's new Pentium microprocessors (sometimes referred to as 586 chips) and PC-based RISC chips (Reduced Instruction Set Chip—a microprocessor designed to do one type of process, such as image manipulation, very efficiently), desktop video-conferencing could experience explosive growth within a few years because of improvements in image quality. New technology also helps to push down the price of existing equipment. Stand-alone systems that would have cost as much as $40,000 only two years ago are now selling for less than $20,000. Hitachi American, Inc. introduced a $15,000 system in 1993.

Businesses and academic groups on the Internet will also find video conferencing more accessible in the near future. In the last year, advances in video compression and the use of a protocol referred to as "packet video"—video images broken into equal-sized data packets and sent to remote sites—have made personal-computer-based video conferencing practical over existing networks. Current software and hardware only generate black-and-white images and are hampered by a slow scan rate (images are captured at a rate per second that is less than necessary for true full-motion action). The equipment is affordably priced, however, and can be used over existing Internet connections without the need for costly dedicated lines. CU-See-Me, developed at Cornell University, is a software program that allows multi-party conferencing. It is being offered at no charge, but it does require the purchase of cameras and video frame-grabber cards (hardware add-ons that allow the computer to translate a video image into a transmittable screen image) for each computer used. In addition to these products, companies are working on more advanced packet-video systems that will provide full-motion color images over existing network links.

Perhaps the most important trend in video conferencing is interconnectivity or compatibility among video-conferencing equipment from different manufacturers. With this interconnectivity, companies can video conference with virtually any business set up to do so, just as they can fax documents to any firm with a fax machine. In general, lower-priced systems are not currently designed for interconnectivity.

Lower prices and technologies that make video conferencing easier than ever to use, will likely entice more businesses. But some bumps may slow the acceptance of this new meeting medium. Anecdotal evidence suggests that some executives find it inconvenient and prone to "glitches," even though they feel comfortable with the technology. In preplanned video conferences, for example, some may find it too much trouble to go to nearby and even in-house video-conferencing rooms to participate in meetings, choosing instead to participate in the meeting by telephone. Because of this reluctance to use video conferencing—avoiding video-conference participation may also be a newly emerging form of executive privilege—and because all participants in a video meeting may not have access to video-conferencing facilities, meetings that include telephone and video participants may become more common.

RESOURCES:

The Meeting Channel
US Sprint Video Group
Atlanta, GA
(800) 877-1108
(meeting and video conferencing services)

Compression Labs, Inc.
San Jose, CA
(408) 435-3000
(video-conferencing systems)

PictureTel Corporation
Danvers, MA
(508) 762-5000
(video-conferencing systems)

Hitachi America Ltd.
Telecommunications Division
Norcross, GA
(404) 446-8820
(telecommunications systems)

Cornell University
Ithaca, NY
(607) 255-3333
(video-conferencing software)
To download free software through
the Internet: use anonymous Ftp
to:gated.cornell.edu Enter "CD to /
PUB/VIDEO" and download most
recent file with "READ ME" in
name.

AT&T Global Business Video
Service
Atlanta, GA
(800) 843-3646
(video-conferencing services)

Yankee Group
Boston, MA
(617) 367-1000
(marketing research)

Desktop Sales

The lower prices for distance-meeting technologies have made way for the next generation of sales calls, "desktop sales." Using desktop video conferencing technology or even Picasso, the still-image phone technology recently developed by AT&T, sales representatives can make sales calls without leaving their desks. Customers save time because person-to-person meetings are done away with. Desktop sales calls could become a major new form of product and service representation.

Desktop sales presentations will include product demonstrations, computerized graphic displays, access to product data, and customer-controlled image manipulation. Interactive sales calls make use of computer-based demonstration programs, multimedia, and interactive publishing formats. A sales person using this approach usually visits the client in person, although delivering disks for the client's use may also work. With this interactive technology available to them, consumers of various products and services may find they need to attend fewer trade shows to stay abreast of developments in their industries.

RESOURCES:

Sales Automation Association
Dearborn, MI
(313) 278-5655
(industry association for business
users of computers, modems, and
software in sales)

Agricultural Trends

The battle against agricultural pests has been waged as long as humans have grown crops. Progress in controlling insects, weeds, and crop diseases has most recently been accomplished with intensive use of chemicals, but they have often proven toxic to the environment, untargeted plants, animals, and people. In the past few decades, alternative approaches have focused on "biologically friendly" controls, such as organic farming methods that deter pests through soil management and natural predators. The combinations of these practices is referred to as "integrated pest management."

In addition, the companies that make agricultural chemicals have been developing a new generation of products that are more effective, target more specific pests and weeds, and are less harmful to the environment. Much of this work is focusing on genetically engineered pesticides and plant varieties. Genetic engineering involves physical and chemical manipulation of genes, combining beneficial DNA segments from one type of organism with those of another.

One example of these new products is Incide from Crop Genetics, which controls corn borers. That pest causes an estimated $500 million damage annually to the corn crop in the U.S. Incide relies on a naturally occurring microorganism that infects and kills the target insect. The EPA has yet to approve the use of this insecticide. Approval and commercial availability could come in two to three years.

FARM FORECASTS

	1994	1984
Total Acres	0.97 billion acres	1.02 million acres
Number of farms	2,076,000	2,334,000
Average farm size	467 acres	436 acres
Average land value (including buildings)	$700 per acre	$801 per acre
Total debt	$152 billion	$204 billion
Gross income	$185 billion	$168 billion
Agricultural exports	$48 billion	$38 billion
Agricultural imports	$25 billion	$19 billion
Government payments to farmers	$7 billion	$8 billion
Number of people living on farms	4,418,000	5,754,000
Fertilizer use	$7.5 billion	$8.4 billion
Pesticide use	$7.5 billion	$4.7 billion

(1984 figures from *Statistical Abstract of the United States*, 1987 and other editions, Agricultural Statistics 1992, USDA)

RESOURCES:

Agritech, Inc.
Columbus, OH
(614) 488-2772
(agricultural research and consulting)

Stewart Agricultural Research
Services, Inc.
Macon, OH
(816) 762-4240
(agricultural research)

Crop Genetics International
Corporation
Hanover, MD
(410) 381-3800
(agricultural research)

Other Pest and Agricultural Trends

ZEBRA MUSSELS Zebra mussels, a mollusk native to the Caspian Sea in eastern Europe, have infested the Great Lakes. These small creatures reproduce in prodigious numbers, driving out desirable native species, clogging intakes for municipal water supplies, and causing other problems. An effective treatment may come from a native-African plant, the African soapberry. Extracts from this plant kill the mussels and also degrade quickly, leaving no toxins behind.

RESOURCES:

University of Toledo Biology Department
Toledo, OH
(419) 537-2065
(zebra mussel research)

FLIES A new product from Biospherics contains a patented material ants and flies eat but cannot digest. The material absorbs water until the insect is blown apart by the pressure.

RESOURCES:

Biospherics, Inc.
Beltsville, MD
(410) 813-2255
(biological research)

WEEDS An extract from sweet potato roots has been found to control weeds such as yellow nutsedge, a major plant pest for many row crops. Researchers at USDA Agricultural Research Service Weed Laboratory are developing this extract for commercial use and experimenting with other naturally occurring plant compounds that inhibit weed growth.

RESOURCES:

USDA Agricultural Research Service
Beltsville, MD
(301) 504-6537
(weed laboratory)

FUNGUS Many types of damaging plant fungi may be controlled with a new fungicide being developed by companies such as ICI Agrochemicals. Derivatives of chemical compounds known as methoxyacrylates found in some toadstools stop respiration in fungal spores. This new substance may even kill fungi that have grown resistant to existing chemical treatments.

RESOURCES:

ICI Agrochemicals, Imperial
Chemical Industries
Wilmington, DE
(302) 886-3000
(agricultural products)

LEAF RUST One of the greatest destructive forces in wheat production is leaf rust, which accounts for as much as $100 million in crop losses in the U.S. annually. After several decades of development, agricultural researchers working at the International Maize and Wheat Improvement Center in El Batan, Mexico, have created a new strain of wheat that is resistant to rust. The new wheat—referred to as Lr34—performs well in warm, moist climates. That means that U.S. farmers outside the typically warm, dry wheat-growing areas may be successful at producing this crop. And the new variety should be a boon to all the nation's wheat growers, most of whom have some degree of wheat rust infestation.

RESOURCES:

Alan Roelfs
USDA Agricultural Research Service
St. Paul, MN
(612) 625-6299
(cereal rust laboratory)

SEXUAL PREFERENCE Agricultural researchers are doing more than battle the natural enemies of farmers. A technology developed recently by the USDA can produce livestock of a predetermined sex. Fluorescent dyes mark chromosomes containing the genetic determiner for males. A laser is then used to detect the sperm that will produce male calves. Female cattle can be artificially inseminated with known-sex sperm either male or female, depending on the breeder's requirements. Animal

Biotechnology Cambridge is the first company to use this process to breed calves. With the sex-sorting technology, both commercial beef and dairy cattle producers can tailor breeding to maximize their profits.

RESOURCES:

USDA Agricultural Research Service
Washington, DC
(202) 720-3656
(government agency involved with
agricultural research and development)

Phones of the Future

Years of gradual development, deregulation, and increasing demand for information have pushed us to the threshold of a new era in telephone use. Although the personal computer is most often touted as the technology of the future for home use, the telephone is more likely to become the gateway to new sources of communications, information, and entertainment. The telephone must change in order to provide this improvement, but unlike computers, the telephone is "user friendly" and familiar to most consumers.

The familiar telephone design will undergo some visible changes in order to accommodate new capabilities. The addition of text or graphics screens will be the most noticeable feature of the new "smart phone." Telephones with data screens are being developed by NYNEX Corporation (in conjunction with Philips Electronics), Northern Telecom Ltd. Canada, Matsushita Electric Industrial Company, and Online Resources & Communications Corporation. Smart phones should pose no threat to the average telephone user. Designs for the devices incorporate simple alphanumeric keypads or touchscreens, along with the typical telephone handset. A simple form of the smart phone is already in use in many areas of the country for caller identification. Customers with this service have a screen that is used to display the phone number of incoming calls.

In the next one to two years, the first generation of the more elaborate smart phones will become available in many metropolitan areas. The telephones themselves are expected to retail for about $500 and be available for rent.

BUSINESS AND
THE ECONOMY

RESOURCES:

Northern Telecom, Inc.
Nashville, TN
(615) 734-4000
(voice and data telecommunications
equipment)

NYNEX Corporation
New York, NY
(212) 370-7400
(regional phone company)

Online Resources &
Communications Corporation
McLean, VA
(703) 442-4646
(online banking services)

Other Telephone Trends

ELECTRONIC DIRECTORIES Bell Atlantic began testing a new electronic telephone directory in mid-1993. Phone users in selected households in northern Virginia were given portable compact disc interactive (CD-I) players containing more than 1 million residential listings, business listings, audio tracks, animated graphics, and display advertising. US West is also developing an electronic directory in conjunction with France Telecom, which was scheduled to be available in Omaha, Minneapolis, and Seattle in 1993. This system is based on one in use by 6 million French households, developed by France Telecom. The US West service will cost users 15 cents per minute. Personal computers will be required for access, or customers can rent specially designed terminals for about $12 per month. The US West system will include residential, business, and government listings, along with maps, display advertising, and information about sales or other business events, which will be updated continuously. Both of these systems will allow callers to search for businesses by key words, proper names, or categories.

RESOURCES:

Bell Atlantic Directory Services
Philadelphia, PA
(215) 963-6000
(telephone and communications
services)

US West
Denver, CO
(800) 879-4357
(telephone and communications
services)

HI-FI CALLS The audio quality of telephone calls has been improving in recent years, thanks to new technology and the use of fiber-optic cables. The latest step in this trend is the marketing of telephones with additional circuitry to improve the quality of voice reproduction. AT&T will also offer its "TrueVoice" system in limited markets beginning in late 1993, with nationwide service scheduled to be available by the end of 1994. This network technology is designed to improve sound quality on all calls. The quality of speaker-phone reception is also benefiting from new technology. The latest models feature enhanced sound, reduced background noise, and fewer perceptible transmission delays.

RESOURCES:

AT&T
New York, NY
(212) 387-5400
(telephone products and services)

LONG-DISTANCE COMPETITION Competition among long-distance carriers should get more intense in the next few years as the Regional Bell Operating Companies (RBOCs), or Baby Bells, vie for regulatory permission to get into the long-distance business. Five of the Baby Bells applied to the Federal Communications Commission in July 1993 to begin offering long-distance service: Bell Atlantic Corporation, BellSouth Corporation, NYNEX Corporation, Pacific Telesis Group, and Southwestern Bell Corporation. Existing long-distance carriers, who are already locked in intense competition, are opposing the expansion of the Baby Bells into long distance, but regulatory approval is expected nonetheless. While it appears inevitable that the Baby Bells will join the ranks of long-distance carriers, they may not pass all regulatory and other hurdles for five or more years. When they do, the increased competition should bring the expected: lower rates for consumers.

RESOURCES:

Bell Atlantic Corporation
Philadelphia, PA
(215) 963-6000
(regional telephone service)

BellSouth Corporation
Atlanta, GA
(404) 529-8611
(regional telephone service)

NYNEX Corporation
New York, NY
(212) 370-7400
(regional telephone service)

Pacific Telesis Group
San Francisco, CA
(415) 394-3000
(regional telephone service)

Southwestern Bell Corporation
San Antonio, TX
(210) 821-4105
(regional telephone service)

SOUND BITES What once was the purview of the media soon may be available to anyone with voice mail. Companies including BellSouth, Bell Atlantic, and Southwestern Bell are experimenting with delivery of news, sports, and weather reports directly to customers' voice-mail systems. The same services are also being made available to personal computer, facsimile machine, and e-mail users. Telephone news services do cost extra. Charges typically are billed with a customer's regular telephone service.

RESOURCES:

BellSouth
Atlanta, GA
(404) 529-8611
(regional telephone service)

Bell Atlantic
Philadelphia, PA
(215) 963-6000
(regional telephone service)

Southwestern Bell
San Antonio, TX
(210) 821-4105
(regional telephone service)

VOICE CONTROL Voice control of telephones may be available shortly. US West is testing voice-controlled dialing in residences and businesses. Other companies are developing voice-control features such as last-call return, call forwarding, and name recognition.

RESOURCES:

US West
Denver, CO
(303) 896-6942
(telephone services)

FREE PHONES FreeFone is an advertising-supported telephone service offered only in Tucson, Arizona. Rather than paying a monthly rate like most telephone customers, subscribers to FreeFone are paid a fee based on the number of calls they make. Each call is preceded by a paid five-second advertisement. Advertisers are charged a flat fee to participate in the service plus an additional fee each time their ad is heard. In addition to advertising exposure, FreeFone advertisers are given specific demographic information about subscribers.

RESOURCES:

FreeFone Information Network
Seattle, WA
(206) 682-3663
(advertising services)

900 FUTURES Telephone services using the 900 area code went into a bit of a slump in 1992. Revenue from these pay-per-use services totaled $550 million, down 40 percent from $975 million in 1991, according to *InfoText* magazine. This backsliding does not mean, however, that 900 services are experiencing a permanent downturn. Rather, they are suffering from the short-term effects of their own success. Factors contributing to the revenue decline of these services include consumer confusion about the difference between 900 numbers and toll-free 800 numbers, negative responses by many consumers to the sex-oriented 900 services, and consumer anger at the services' rate structures.

But developers of 900 services are looking to shake off their negative images, with an expanded repertoire of services. These may include linking interactive computer and voice-based information services with customers; accessing service centers for consumer products, computers, and software; allowing more direct pay-per-use of computer bulletin boards and similar online data services; connecting customers with fax publishing centers; and implementing special sales and marketing events.

RESOURCES:

InfoText
published by Advanstar
Communications
Santa Ana, CA
(714) 513-8400

800 TRENDS Competition among companies providing 800 toll-free telephone numbers has lowered prices, increased availability, and whetted the appetite of a large new market for this type of service. Personal 800 numbers are fast becoming a new type of status symbol, listed on business cards much like telex numbers used to be and fax numbers are now. At the end of 1992, there were an estimated 1.5 million households with personal 800 numbers. Primary nonbusiness users so far have been families with children away at college, business travelers, and professionals who spend a lot of time away from home. While 800 numbers have long been used by large firms and mail-order companies, small businesses and home-based enterprises are likely to take advantage of lower rates for 800 service. What's next? How about unlisted 800 numbers?

RESOURCES:

Yankee Group
Boston, MA
(617) 367-1000
(market research)

NEW CODES The use of telephones is one example of how difficult it is to predict how people and societies will change over time. Until the 1980s, it was believed that phone use would increase no faster than the general population. After all, how many phones can a person use? But the arrival of fax machines, computer modems, cellular telephones, 800 lines, 900 lines, and home offices have destroyed this logic. An estimated 7,500 new telephone numbers are ordered every day—2.7 million new numbers per year. Under the current system of 150 area codes, only about 7.8 million different phone numbers can be assigned in a single area and the nation has just about reached the limit.

In 1995, Bellcore, the company created by the Baby Bells to oversee the country's area-code system, is expected to expand the current system of area codes. As many as 640 new area codes will be created between 1995 and 2000. All area codes now have middle digits of "1" or "0"; new codes will use additional digits. One new area code already planned for 1994 will split a portion of the Philadelphia area's 215 code into the new code 610, effective in January.

RESOURCES:

Bellcore Bell Communications
Research, Inc.
Livingston, NJ
(201) 740-4324
(telephone systems research and
engineering)

Cellular-Telephone Trends

Cellular-telephone service is now available in almost every corner of
the U.S. At least one company is providing service in each of the nation's
734 cellular-phone marketing areas. In competing markets, most companies are focusing on boosting market share, and a few are looking
skyward to expand their cellular business. Satellite cellular service is in
the works and may be introduced as early as 1994. This technology will
allow cellular phone-system operators to cover more territory with less
equipment, provide more "seamless" service throughout a region, and
deliver more kinds of information, including computer data. Companies that are planning to get into satellite service include American
Mobile Satellite Corporation; Ellipsat, a division of Mobile Communications Holding; Iridium, which is owned by Motorola; Loral Qualcomm
Satellite Services; Orbital Communications, a division of Orbital Sciences; and TRW Space and Electronics Group.

Some experts believe satellite cellular service is a case of "too much,
too soon." They do not think consumers are ready to spend the $2,500
satellite phones are expected to cost, nor pay the higher per-minute
cost. And even if some cellular phone users are willing to pay for satellite service, there are unlikely to be enough to support more than one
such service. On top of that, ground-based cellular service is constantly
improving with the use of fiber optics and high-density transmissions.
The result may be that the less-expensive conventional cellular service
is every bit as good as satellite service.

Support for ground-based cellular systems is also coming from the
improving strength of some companies, particularly McCaw Cellular. In
1993, AT&T purchased a 33 percent share of this business, substantially

boosting its capability to expand its market share, develop new technology, and create an interconnected system of cellular-phone regions.

RESOURCES:

Ellipsat Corporation
Washington, DC
(202) 466-4488
(cellular-telephone services)

Iridium, Inc.
Washington, DC
(202) 371-6880
(satellite communications)

TRW Space & Technology
Corporation
Redondo Beach, CA
(310) 812-4616
(satellite communications)

Qualcomm, Inc.
San Diego, CA
(619) 587-1121
(digital wireless communications)

Orbital Sciences Corporation
Dulles, VA
(703) 406-5000
(space communications systems)

Cellular Business
published by Intertec Publishing
Company
Overland Park, KS
(913) 341-1300

Other Cellular Trends

CELLULAR PAY PHONES Telephone companies will be installing more pay phones that use wireless cellular transmissions. These units can be installed in places not normally served by telephone lines—parks, hiking trails, highway rest stops, outdoor events, and even public transportation vehicles. Taking a cue from the telephones installed in most commercial airliners in the past few years, some cellular companies are rushing to put units in taxis, ferries, buses, and commuter trains.

RESOURCES:

Cellular Telecommunications
Industry Association
Washington, DC
(202) 785-0081
(industry association for businesses
involved with cellular
communications)

Cellular One, Inc.
Westwood, MA
(617) 462-4000
(cellular communications)

CELLULAR SMART PHONES New cellular telephones from Motorola can receive text messages sent from personal computers. Digital messages up to 14 characters long are displayed on a small screen built into the cellular telephones. This service was first offered by US West Cellular and Sprint in mid-1993. Users pay about $10 per month, in addition to regular cellular charges.

The Motorola system uses a hybrid analog/digital system. Other new cellular technology will rely completely on digital data. Cellular Digital Packet Data is a new technology developed by Bell Atlantic, McCaw Cellular Communications, and Ameritech. This technology transmits digital signals to and from cellular phones. Digitized signals can transmit text as well as voice signals. McCaw has announced the implementation of the new technology in half of its market area, which should be completed by the end of 1993 and the remainder by mid-1994.

RESOURCES:

US West Cellular
Denver, CO
(303) 368-8778
(cellular-telephone services)

Sprint Corporation
Westwood, KS
(913) 624-6000
(local and long-distance
telecommunications services)

McCaw Cellular Communications
Company
Kirkland, WA
(206) 827-4500
(cellular-telephone systems)

LOW-POWER CELLULAR With low-power cellular service, people within the confines of a college campus, factory, or other such compound can send and receive regular telephone calls as well as messages generated within the confined area. One example is the Freeset system designed by Ericsson North America for confined geographical environments with a large number of phone users and a high volume of calls. The first test of its system began in 1993 at the Long Beach campus of California State University.

RESOURCES:

Ericsson North America, Inc.
Richardson, TX
(214) 669-9900
(telephone equipment)

LOST-AND-FOUND CELLULAR TrackMobile has developed a new cellular telephone design that could make these mobile devices more accessible to the mass market. For about $20, consumers can purchase these limited-function phones, which feature no dials. Monthly fees of about $12 and additional charges per call will allow anyone to have a cellular phone. This system utilizes operators to place calls, which allows the phones to also be marketed as emergency communicators. By pressing one button, the caller is connected to an operator or, for an additional fee, full-time private security forces. An added feature: callers can be located upon request by a computerized system that pinpoints locations from triangulation of nearby cellular transmission sites.

RESOURCES:

TrackMobile, Inc.
San Diego, CA
(619) 235-6085
(cellular-telephone products
and services)

HEALTH AND MEDICINE

HEALTH AND MEDICINE

Hospitals are trying to stay in business as occupancy declines, and consumers are trying to stay out of the doctor's office by trying some unusual remedies and health-enhancers. In 1994, researchers will be trying improved treatments for migraine headaches and new diet drugs, and testing vaccines for certain cancers, Lyme disease, and poison ivy.

The Business
of Health

More and more potential hospital patients are becoming outpatients.
The average occupancy rate of U.S. hospitals is now about 60 percent.
That means more than one-third of hospital beds are unused in a given
year. In 1983, the occupancy rate was about 75 percent. Declining use
of hospital bed space is a trend that is expected to continue as a result
of improvements in outpatient procedures, early diagnoses, more effective drug therapies, and pressure from insurance companies to reduce
hospital stays.

The overall effect on the hospital industry will be a decline in construction of new facilities, merging of some local hospitals, cooperation
between facilities in the same communities to reduce redundant departments and expensive services, redesign of some existing hospitals
and hospital wards for administrative and outpatient services, and the
reuse of some facilities for specialized care such as geriatric services.

By 1995, the decline in inpatient hospital use may slow or plateau,
as the market experiences the net effects of some hospital closings. In
many cities, however, competition and politics are proving inefficient
partners in responding to the trend of fewer hospital inpatients. Not-
for-profit facilities, which account for about 75 percent of all hospitals
in the country, are often slow to respond to these changes, while most
for-profit hospitals have already adjusted. In the five-year period ended
in 1991, 551 community hospitals were closed or merged because of a
decline in use, or about 10 percent of all hospitals. But construction of
new facilities offset this decline by half.

American Hospital Association
Chicago, IL
(312) 280-6000

(industry association of hospitals
and other health care institutions)

Health Care Computerization

FORMS Software to make billing more efficient includes pre-created forms for insurance claims and automated payments. Standardization among insurers is increasingly common and will become more so with added use of networking, allowing the same information to be easily shared by different companies. Another advance is the creation of centralized patient data centers, commercial operations that maintain patients' computerized files for individual doctors.

Patient Record Institute
American Health Information
Management Association
Chicago, IL
(312) 787-2672
(industry group working to create
networking standards for medical
forms)

Medical Records Institute
Newton, MA
(617) 964-3923
(industry association for personnel
involved with medical
documentation)

PORTABLE DATA Personal-medical-information storage systems are being developed to facilitate scanning of medical records between doctors, clinics, hospitals, and insurance agencies. One example is "smart cards," credit-card-sized electronic identification cards on which medical records are encoded. Smart cards are being touted by the Clinton administration as it studies health care reform. Limitations in memory may curtail their use however. Other technologies, such as optically recorded cards, can hold considerably more information, including X-ray and MRI images. Even these cards lack sufficient storage for long-term use, however. Add to that the fact that smart-card and optical-card scanners are not cheap—$400 and $3,000 respectively—and options like centralized patient data centers (see above) begin to look more attractive. These centers have large-scale data storage capabilities and can transmit unlimited amounts of patient information, including images.

RESOURCES:

Smart Card Monthly
published by Smart Card Concepts
Montara, CA
(415) 728-3920
(industry publication about smart cards, memory cards, and optical cards)

AT&T Smart Cards
Somerset, NJ
(800) 854-6620
(smart-card research and development)

VOICE PROCESSING Voice processing will be increasingly used in hospitals to speed up and standardize entry of patient information. Computer systems from Kurzweil Applied Intelligence are already in use in hospitals. Specialized applications include medical record entry, emergency room information, radiology, and pathology.

RESOURCES:

Kurzweil Applied Intelligence, Inc.
Waltham, MA
(617) 893-5151
(Voice-recognition computer systems)

REMOTE LINKS Telecommunications links will allow more data sharing among labs, hospitals, and doctors including patient records, test results, and patient monitoring. Simple connections using telephone lines, modems, and personal computers are already in use throughout the industry. Coming soon will be more complex connections involving high-speed data lines, transmissions of medical images such as dental and medical X rays, and increasing use of the Internet. The advantages of the Internet are the many academic and medical institutions with connections already established on this network and the high speed and data volume capability necessary for transmitting digital images.

RESOURCES:

The American Medical Informatics Association
Bethesda, MD
(301) 657-1291

(industry association of doctors, scientists, engineers, administrators, and computer professionals using advanced-technology systems)

HEALTH AND MEDICINE

Future
Scanning

Diagnostic scanners such as Magnetic Resonance Imaging (MRI) are a source of technological progress in the U.S., as well as political controversy. Progress is represented by improvements in imaging methods, while the controversy arises from the current high cost for diagnosis with this equipment.

More than 3,500 MRIs are currently in use in the U.S., as are more than 6,000 worldwide. In most major U.S. cities, there are at least 20 of these machines. By comparison there are only 20 in all of Canada. Currently, there are 8 million scans annually in the U.S., compared with fewer than 3 million in 1987. MRI scans account for an estimated $6 billion in annual medical charges.

Most criticism of MRI use is aimed at its cost, not its effectiveness. The figure most often cited for MRI scanning is $1,000 per scan. This figure represents an industry average from 1988 when there were half as many machines in use. In 1991, the average charge in the U.S. was about $700. Within the next few years, the price should drop to $500 as a result of competition among hospitals and clinics providing the service. The competition is especially fierce in major metropolitan areas.

MRIs have provided a major leap forward from diagnoses performed by X rays, a technology that will be 100 years old in 1995. The primary benefit of MRIs is their noninvasive nature. Images are created by using magnetic fields to produce resonance, or molecular vibrations. The electrical signal this resonance produces creatures a picture of body tissue.

In the U.S., MRIs are routinely used for diagnosing soft-tissue injuries, tumors, and head trauma. The current generation of machines in use relies on mechanical technology that has been in use for more than five years. Successive generations of computer software have helped create increasingly detailed images from the same machines.

One new MRI development is magnification, or MRI microscopy. With this technology, which is already in use in several labs, subjects as small as 10 microns in size can be viewed. A human hair is about 100 microns in diameter. The result should mean that the process of laboratory testing will be faster because results can be noted immediately. A reduction in the number of laboratory animals required for research is also possible. Instead of destroying test animals to examine them, the results of experiments can be determined without harming the animals.

Another MRI development is the creation of three-dimensional images. This technique is expected to improve the efficiency and effectiveness of some types of operations by allowing surgeons to "preview" a result. The technology has already been tried at Boston's Children's Hospital. It may also be used to guide surgeons during delicate brain operations.

MRI technology may soon be used to monitor brain response. Unlike positron emission tomography (PET)—currently used for studying brain reactions—researchers can conduct MRI brain scans without injecting subjects with radioactive isotopes. One such MRI application under development uses the computer functions of the scanner to diminish the effects of movement, such as the beating of the heart, on image quality. The computer synchronizes non-MRI readings from an electroencephalograph (EEG) with scanned information.

A technological cousin of MRI is Adaptive Current Tomography (ACT), which uses electrical current to create images of body tissues. A low, nondangerous current is run through the body. Since each tissue type offers a different level of resistance, an image can be created based on electrical impedance measurements.

MRIs are large stationary pieces of equipment, but the images they produce are being sent to remote locations via telecommunications links. They then are viewed on high-resolution monitors by doctors like those at the University of Maryland Medical School in Baltimore. This teleradiology technique can also be used to transmit other electronically produced images.

Even though MRI is a relatively new technology, the current systems already are being supplanted by even more sophisticated scanners. These elaborate machines cost more, so when used for diagnoses, patients will be charged more. Today's scanners are far from obsolete, however. They are likely to end up in smaller markets that previously did not have the technology. In places where both the new and old scanners are in use, equipment choice will most likely be based on the image detail required. All in all, competition among providers of these scanning services should continue to force patient charges down.

The same computer advances that are improving the quality of MRI images are doing the same for ultrasound. Ultrasound, too, is benefiting from improvements in computer science. Ultrasound equipment is already a widely used diagnostic tool—only X-ray equipment is more commonplace in U.S. hospitals. The next wave of technology should mean even more detailed images. These computerized ultrasound images not only feature more detail, they can be transmitted instantly to remote locations because they are created and stored as digital images.

RESOURCES:

Computerized Medical Imaging Society
Washington, DC
(202) 687-2121
(industry association for medical personnel involved with radiological diagnostic procedure)

Society for Magnetic Resonance Imaging
Chicago, IL
(312) 751-2590
(industry association for doctors and scientists using neuroimaging technology in research)

American Society of Neuroimaging
Minneapolis, MN
(612) 378-7240
(industry association for doctors and physicists using X rays, ultrasound, MRIs, and other technology for diagnosis and treatment of disease)

New Horizons

ANTISENSE Biotechnologists are creating a new group of drugs from compounds known as antisense agents. These substances utilize specific molecules to treat diseases such as cancer, thus reducing the side effects associated with many cancer treatments. Antisense drugs employ protein-like chemicals to trigger reactions from DNA within cells, turning on the production of beneficial cells and turning off the production of disease-producing cells. The drugs may be effective in treating cancer, HIV-related infections, diabetes, and arthritis. Clinical trials and patents mark progress for treatments for leukemia, septic shock, and genital warts.

RESOURCES:

Genta, Inc.
San Diego, CA
(619) 455-2700
(anticode oligonucleotides research and development for treatment of leukemia)

Lynx Therapeutics, Inc.
Foster City, CA
(415) 570-6667
(research and development of pharmaceuticals for treatment of leukemia)

Isis Pharmaceuticals, Inc.
Carlsbad, CA
(619) 931-9200
(anticode oligonucleotides research and development for treatment of genital warts)

FETAL CELLS Progress in treating Parkinson's disease with fetal cell implants has spurred research into using the treatment for other ailments, including as a preventative for scarring after surgery. The therapy works by injecting fetal cells, whose characteristics are not yet determined, into a patient made dysfunctional by a disease like Parkinson's. In their new environment, the cells develop new functions as they mature, rejuvenating the function of an organ.

RESOURCES:

Biochemical and Biophysical Research
Communications
published by Academic Press
San Diego, CA
(619) 230-1840

Molecular Brain Research
published by Elsevier
Amsterdam, The Netherlands
and New York, NY
(212) 989-5800

FIELD EFFECTS Public controversy aside, medical research has yet to turn up definitive evidence that electromagnetic fields (EMFs) cause physical harm. New research, however, may soon disclose what previous research has not: a causal link. Research published in 1992 and 1993 links the fluctuating magnetic fields associated with EMFs to disruption in the normal cancer-fighting activity of melatonin, a hormone secreted by the pineal gland. Melatonin is involved with the aging process, regulates heart rhythms, suppresses tumor growth, and possibly contributes to stress. Emerging EMF data points to proximity to the source of the field as a major factor in inducing physical harm.

RESOURCES:

International Journal of Neuroscience
published by Gordon and Breach
Science Publishers
New York, NY
(212) 206-8900

Journal of Cellular Biochemistry
published by John Wiley and Sons,
Inc. Journals
New York, NY
(212) 850-6000

PREDICTING DIABETES A major project is underway to develop a test to detect the onset of diabetes in healthy, but at-risk, people. The program relies on a blood test that detects and measures levels of antibodies produced when islets—the cells in the pancreas that make insulin—are being destroyed. Researchers believe the destruction of islets predates the onset of diabetes by one or more years. Identification of this early sign could be followed by preventative treatments to delay the onset of the disease.

RESOURCES:

Barbara Davis Center for Childhood
Diabetes
Denver, CO
(303) 270-8796
(research organization studying diabetes)

CANCER VACCINES Many research projects are underway to develop vaccines for cancer, but no significant breakthroughs have been reported. One of the most promising potential vaccines is GM-CSF (granulocyte-macrophage colony stimulating factor), which has been successful in preventing melanoma in mice. Testing on humans may begin by late 1993 or early 1994.

RESOURCES:

Genetics Institute, Inc.
Cambridge, MA
(617) 876-1170
(biopharmaceuticals research
and development)

Immunex Corporation
Seattle, WA
(206) 587-0430
(immune system pharmaceuticals)

American Cancer Society
Atlanta, GA
(404) 320-3333
(national organization involved
with research, education, early
detection, and treatment of cancer)

FREE-RADICAL ATTACK The latest popular battlefront in the medical research industry revolves around the development of products to reduce free radicals in the human body. These compounds, distinguished by their molecular instability and propensity to cause cell damage, are becoming a popular culprit in the hunt for the causes and functioning of many diseases, including cancer, heart disease, AIDS, strokes, and others. Free-radical treatments target the extra oxygen component that makes free radicals unstable. Topping the list of free-radical treatments are vitamins E and C, which are potent natural antioxidants. For several years, momentum in the vitamin and food-supplement industry has been building to promote the effectiveness of these compounds and others at fighting free radicals. Another nonprescription antioxidant that is gaining popularity in the health-food market is Pycnogenol from Source Naturals, a trademarked nutritional supplement developed from proanthocyanidins, naturally occurring substances found in some pine-tree bark.

The mainstream medical products industry has only recently jumped on this bandwagon, but it should be getting in the act soon with its own free-radical treatments. Aside from medically prescribed doses of vitamins, some companies are rushing to develop more powerful antioxidants as preventative therapy for everything from AIDS to tuberculosis.

RESOURCES:

Cardiovascular Research
published by British Medical
Journal Publishing Group
London, England
(071) 387-4499

Chemical Research in Toxicology
published by The American
Chemical Society
Washington, DC
(800) 333-9511

Threshold Enterprises, Ltd.
Scotts Valley, CA
(408) 438-6851
(manufacturer of nutritional
supplements)

CHEMICAL EVOLUTION A new drug-development method can produce research results in a few weeks that would take years using traditional research techniques. Directed molecular evolution (also referred to as applied molecular evolution) takes compounds that hold promise as pharmaceuticals and exposes them to a series of chemical tests that eliminate molecules that do not achieve the designated result. This "survival of the fittest" process continues until the most effective compound is derived. Gilead Sciences, Inc. has used molecular evolution to develop an anticlotting drug from a DNA segment known to neutralize natural clotting factors in the blood. Companies that are employing molecular evolution in their drug-development research include NeXagen Inc., Selectide Inc., and Isis Pharmaceuticals Inc.

RESOURCES:

Gilead Sciences, Inc.
Foster City, CA
(415) 574-3000
(nucleotide-based pharmaceuticals
research and development)

NeXagen, Inc.
Boulder, CO
(303) 444-5893
(biopharmaceuticals research and
development)

Isis Pharmaceuticals Inc.
Carlsbad, CA
(619) 931-9200
(antisense oligonucleotides research
and development)

Selectide, Inc.
Tucson, AZ
(602) 575-8040
(pharmaceutical manufacturing)

Other Health Care Trends

PRIVATE SNIPPING Vasectomies are becoming less and less involved for doctors and patients, thanks to the advent of micro-methods. In a microvasectomy procedure, a tiny opening is made in the testis, and sterilization is accomplished by cutting and tying off the vas, or sperm tube. This procedure can be done on an outpatient basis, one of the reasons it has become so popular in recent years. The next development in the miniaturization of this process is the soon-to-arrive Vasocclude, a tiny metal clip that should replace the surgical severing now required to block sperm flow. An added advantage for the clip: the procedure can be easily reversed, restoring reproduction capability.

RESOURCES:

Planned Parenthood Federation of
America
New York, NY
(212) 541-7800
(national organization providing
education, information, and medical
services related to contraception,
abortion, sterilization, and
infertility)

Association for Voluntary Surgical
Contraception
New York, NY
(212) 561-8000
(national organization providing
education, information, and
professional training in the use of
surgical contraceptive methods)

FREEZE-DRIED BLOOD One answer to the problem of keeping adequate supplies of blood on hand for surgery and emergencies may be freeze-drying. Fresh blood is normally refrigerated but can be kept for only six weeks. Where refrigeration is unavailable, blood must be used in a few hours. The freeze-drying process, which is not yet approved by the FDA for use, removes the liquid components of blood without damaging cell membranes.

RESOURCES:

Cryopharm Corporation
Pasadena, CA
(818) 793-1040
(research and development in the
preservation of blood products)

PATCH BURNOUT Nicotine-patch sales are slowing after an initial boom. Most major patch makers reported declining sales in the first part of 1993, and some industry analysts now suggest that the market may have already peaked. Problems facing the patch include loss of interest as this novel treatment becomes more commonplace, a declining number of smokers, and the difficulty of achieving successful results without behavioral modification therapy.

RESOURCES:

American Druggist
published by the Hearst Corporation
New York, NY
(212) 297-9680
(industry publication)

CARPAL TUNNEL INSIGHT Spurred by a growing rash of office injuries due to repetitive motion disorder and one form of it, carpal tunnel syndrome (CTS), medical organizations are beginning to reevaluate this ubiquitous ailment of white-collar workers. More than 100,000 cases of repetitive motion disorder are reported annually, with about 10 percent of those cases being classified as CTS. CTS is thought to be caused by long-term repetition of limited motions such as keyboard entry, and involves pain, weakness, and decreased flexibility in the limbs or digits affected. These figures are thought to represent only a fraction of workers. Many respond to the characteristic pain in the wrist and arms with self-diagnosis and in some cases, nonmainstream medical treatment (see below). At least half of the workers diagnosed with CTS do not actually have the nerve damage that typically marks the pain as being caused by CTS. These sufferers are thought to have a form of pre-CTS, which is characterized by pain from swollen tendons and muscles. When addressed at this stage by a change in work habits or time away from the job, sufferers may be able to stop the onset of the disease and avoid the standard treatment—surgery.

RESOURCES:

National Institute of Occupational
Safety and Health
Cincinnati, OH
(800) 356-4674
(government agency involved with
work-place safety and occupational
injuries)

American Physical Therapy
Association
Alexandria, VA
(703) 684-2782
(industry association for physical
therapists)

MENDING MENOPAUSE Aging baby boomers are turning a previously private topic into commonplace conversation. Menopause is coming out of the closet, and along the way, it is providing profit potential for the medical industry from pharmaceutical makers to psychiatrists. Menopause may become the next "pet" condition of the decade, after depression. At the front of commercial developments for menopausal women are products that relieve vaginal dryness. Products formerly marketed as vaginal lubricants and sexual aids are now being reintroduced as vaginal moisturizers and marketed to the new menopausal generation. In 1992, the sales of personal lubricants increased 30 percent over the previous year and totaled $40 million.

RESOURCES:

Society for Menstrual Cycle
Research
Scottsdale, AZ
(602) 451-9731
(industry association for medical
personnel and scientists involved in
the study of the menstrual cycle)

North American Menopause Society
Cleveland, OH
(216) 844-3334
(industry association for medical
personnel and scientists involved in
the study of the climacteric period
in men and women)

BONE-MARROW BARGAINS Bone-marrow transplants are one of the cancer treatments for which insurance companies most often refuse to pay. The procedure, in which a patient's immune system is intentionally depressed before healthy bone-marrow cells are introduced to stimulate production of healthy cells, is experimental. More important to insurance companies, however, it is expensive. The treatments typically cost $150,000 or more. Progress is being made in reducing these costs, primarily by shortening hospital stays for such patients. This can be accomplished through improved infection-fighting drugs and monitoring recuperating patients at home. Medical researchers are also working to improve transplants by developing new sources of bone-marrow cells, through bioengineering and isolation of these cells from blood samples.

RESOURCES:

National Bone Marrow Donor
Registry
Minneapolis, MN
(612) 627-5800
(national organization of doctors
and scientists providing research,
information, and support for bone-
marrow use in medicine)

HOUSE CALLS The number of doctors making house calls is increasing. House calls have been a service few physicians provide in recent decades, and when available, the service is often prohibitively expensive. But today, more doctors are making house calls as part of a growing trend—the practice of family medicine. More physicians are offering this primary care because of the nation's unexpectedly high birth rate—the echo baby boom—and to serve elderly patients who are seeking less expensive forms of care than those available through hospitals. Also, more beginning doctors are choosing this option because they seek personal satisfaction from their medical careers that is not offered by clinical practice or specialization.

RESOURCES:

American Academy of Family
Physicians
Kansas City, MO
(816) 333-9700
(independent association of medical
professionals in family practice)

American Medical Association
Chicago, IL
(312) 464-4818
(industry association of medical
professionals)

EARLY WARNING SYSTEM The Centers for Disease Control and Prevention (CDC), part of the Public Health Service, is planning to set up ten or more surveillance centers to identify and study outbreaks of disease. At least a few of these centers are expected to be located at major entry ports to the U.S., such as Miami and New York City, cities where travelers and immigrants often first expose others to viruses, microbes, and disease-causing parasites. Although these centers are expected to keep an eye on new diseases, they will also track well-known diseases such as tuberculosis, measles, and polio.

RESOURCES:

Centers for Disease Control
Atlanta, GA
(404) 639-3286
(government agency involved with
research, education, detection, and
control of diseases)

Drug Trends

The manufacture and marketing of generic prescription drugs has become a major part of the pharmaceutical industry. Annual sales of generic drugs are now about $9 billion and increasing at about 10 percent per year. Generics account for an estimated 25 percent of the total prescription-drug sales market. Brand-name prescription drugs doing about $10 billion in annual sales will lose their patent protection each year through 1995. Over the course of the decade, brand-name drug sales of $16 billion could be affected by generic equivalents. Increased consumer demand for lower drug prices will also impel more generic versions. By the year 2000, one projection has generics increasing to 33 percent of all drug sales.

Competition from the major drug companies, however, will increasingly limit growth in the production of generics. Even as patents expire for some brands, research and development by the companies holding the patents is expected to produce refined versions, which are likely to have improved efficacy, a wider range of use, and more effective dosages. Several drug companies have also chosen to compete with generic manufacturers by producing generic equivalents of their own formerly patented drugs. Companies that are doing this include Merck and Company (through a new subsidiary, West Point Pharma).

RESOURCES:

Merck and Company
West Point Pharma Division
West Point, PA
(215) 652-5000
(pharmaceutical manufacturer)

Natwest Investment Banking Group
New York, NY
(212) 440-8300
(industry analysis for investment)

Generic Pharmaceutical Industry
Association
New York, NY
(212) 683-1881
(industry association for
manufacturers, distributors, and
retailers of generic drugs)

New Drugs

CHOLERA VACCINE A new oral cholera vaccine is faring well in initial clinical trials. The drug has few side effects.

RESOURCES:

University of Maryland
School of Medicine
Baltimore, MD
(410) 706-3100
(cholera-vaccine research)

POISON-IVY VACCINE This menace to the epidermis may have met its match if a new vaccine is successful. The vaccine inhibits the effect of urushiol, the compound in the plant responsible for the rash it gives humans. The drug should be subjected to clinical tests soon.

RESOURCES:

Stiefel Laboratories, Inc.
Coral Gables, FL
(305) 443-3807
(poison-ivy-vaccine research and
development)

FLU VACCINE A new flu vaccine that can be administered through the nose may be available by 1996. The new nose drops have been developed by Wyeth-Ayerst Laboratories.

RESOURCES:

Wyeth-Ayerst Laboratories
St. David, PA
(215) 688-4400
(flu-vaccine research and
development)

LYME-DISEASE VACCINE Clinical trials for a vaccine protecting against Lyme disease have begun, with preliminary results expected by the end of 1994. Lyme disease is an inflammatory disorder thought to be spread by ticks.

RESOURCES:

Connaught Laboratories, Inc.
Swiftwater, PA
(717) 839-7187
(Lyme-disease-vaccine research and development)

PROGRESS FOR MIGRAINES Migraines are mainstream: an estimated 16 to 18 million Americans suffer from these debilitating headache attacks. Many doctors treat migraines with a traditional counterattack of old and new pain medicines and tranquilizers. New drugs coming on the scene include Imitrex from Glaxo. Imitrex causes serotonin—a neurotransmitter—to bind to receptors in the brain to block migraine pain. Imitrex is now only administered as an injection, but FDA approval of a tablet form of the drug may come within another year. The tablets are already available in Canada. A drug similar to Imitrex is DHE from Sandoz, which also is limited to administration by injection. A nasal spray form of DHE is awaiting approval from the FDA and could be available as early as the end of 1993.

RESOURCES:

American Pharmaceutical
Association
Washington, DC
(202) 628-4410
(industry association of pharmacists and other individuals involved in research and supply of drugs)

Glaxo, Inc.
Research Triangle Park, NC
(919) 248-2100
(pharmaceutical manufacturer of Imitrex)

Sandoz Pharmaceuticals
Corporation
East Hanover, NJ
(201) 503-7500
(pharmaceutical manufacturer of DHE)

DIET DRUGS Over-the-counter diet pills are suffering from a double blow: consumers are buying less of them and the FDA has recently banned 111 ingredients used in many of these products. Although few new over-the-counter diet drugs are expected in coming years, new prescription help for obesity is reportedly on the way. Chemical compounds found to aid weight loss in clinical trials include phentermine, registered under the trade name Lonamin by Fisons; dexfenfluramine, made by Interneuron Pharmaceutical; orlistat, from Hoffmann-LaRoche; fenfluramine produced by Robins as Pondimin; and fluoxetine, which is trademarked as Prozac. That drug, made by Eli Lilly & Company, is now widely used for the treatment of depression. Another anti-depression drug, sertraline, also holds promise for aiding weight loss. Pfizer markets sertraline as Zoloft.

Some or all of these compounds could be commercially available in one to three years, and it is clearly a possibility that these drugs may experience a boom in popularity like that of Valium in the 1970s and Prozac today. New diet drugs may also precipitate a wave of prescription drug abuse, overprescription, and street resale.

RESOURCES:

Fisons Corporation
Rochester, NY
(716) 475-9000
(pharmaceuticals for control of diet)

Interneuron Pharmaceutical, Inc.
Lexington, MA
(617) 861-8444
(pharmaceuticals for control of diet)

Hoffmann-LaRoche, Inc.
Nutley, NJ
(201) 235-5000
(pharmaceuticals for control of diet)

Eli Lilly & Company
Indianapolis, IN
(317) 276-2000
(pharmaceuticals for control of diet)

Pfizer, Inc.
New York, NY
(212) 573-2323
(pharmaceuticals for control of diet)

A. H. Robins Company, Inc.
Richmond, VA
(804) 257-2000
(pharmaceuticals for control of diet)

GLAUCOMA TREATMENT A new drug may provide a more effective treatment for glaucoma. Ethacrynic acid, a compound originally developed as a diuretic, is being tested for its ability to decrease intraocular pressure. The excessive pressure in the fluid behind the cornea associated with glaucoma damages the optic nerve and often results in blindness. Drugs currently used to combat glaucoma restrict the inflow of fluid and must be taken daily. Ethacrynic acid works by improving the eye's natural ability to drain fluid and may have to be administered only once a year.

RESOURCES:

American Optometric Association
St. Louis, MO
(314) 991-4100
(industry association for optometric
professionals)

Telor Ophthalmic Pharmaceuticals
Inc.
Woburn, MA
(617) 937-0393
(pharmaceuticals for eye disease)

Research to Prevent Blindness
New York, NY
(212) 752-4333
(national organization involved
with researching causes, prevention,
and treatment of eye diseases that
cause blindness)

WAR ON MS Progress toward a cure or treatment for multiple sclerosis includes five drugs currently undergoing clinical tests on humans and at least six more that should be tested soon. The Chiron Corporation, in conjunction with Berlex Laboratories, Inc., has already conducted tests of Betaseron, and the companies have applied for FDA approval to market the drug. Beta interferon, the chemical name for Betaseron, has reportedly reduced the frequency with which the disease flares up in those who have it and reduces the incidence of brain lesions. A related compound, alpha interferon, has also shown promise as an MS treatment in animal tests.

RESOURCES:

National Multiple Sclerosis Society
New York, NY
(212) 986-3240
(national organization promoting
research and education into the
causes and treatment of MS)

Berlex Laboratories Inc.
Wayne, NJ
(201) 694-4100
(pharmaceutical manufacturer)

Chiron Corporation
Emeryville, CA
(510) 655-8730
(DNA technology and vaccines
research and development)

New-Age
Alternatives

A recent survey published in the *New England Journal of Medicine* concluded that about one-third of Americans use some form of alternative medicine and spend $14 billion annually on products and services not recognized by the medical establishment.

As the enormous baby-boom generation hits middle age and experiences the health problems of aging, it should spend more and more on both traditional and alternative healing practices. In the past decade, alternative medicine has gone through fads such as crystal therapy, channeling, and astrology. Like most healing practices tried in this country in the past century, these have faded in popularity, but have not disappeared entirely. Alternative healing fads are often based on practices rooted in ancient cultures; some synthesize elements of several practices.

Ancient traditions of the Orient are currently enjoying popularity in alternative-medicine circles. Among these are acupressure, acupuncture, and Chi Kung, or traditional Chinese healing. In modern Chinese society, Chi Kung is called Qi Gong. It is a system that involves exercises and meditation to improve and maintain physical and mental health.

Another ancient, but less accepted practice, has also appeared on the alternative medicine scene—witchcraft. Forms of witchcraft from native cultures in Africa and the Americas are being explored, especially by those with no roots in the cultures that originated them. Shamanism, earth-based religions, magical healing, fetishes, charms, rituals, and chanting are all part of this trend.

The more outlandish practices associated with witchcraft and other fringe practices are likely to help make once-little-known treatments seem conservative, thus increasing their acceptance among alternative-medicine adherents. Long-standing healing methods that are growing in popularity include Rolfing, massage therapy, homeopathy, and transpersonal psychology. And many new treatments are emerging, including aromatherapy, therapeutic sound, and Tibetan Point Holding. These may establish a new baseline for the truly strange among alternative- healing practices, although many dabblers in these areas do not abandon western medicine while doing so.

Traditional medicine has long known of the tendency for some people to respond to treatment with an inert substance, a placebo, when they believe the substance is really an effective medicine. Some research physicians have shown that the placebo effect is stronger in those with higher education levels. Since the baby-boom generation has the highest share of college graduates, the future market for alternative remedies may be poised for growth.

RESOURCES:

Magical Blend
published by Magical Blend
Publishers
San Francisco, CA
(415) 673-1001

New Age Journal
published by Rising Star
Associates, Ltd.
Brighton, MA
(617) 926-0200

Alternative Healing: The Complete
A-Z Guide to Over 160 Different
Alternative Therapies
by Mark Kastner and Hugh
Burroughs
Halcyon Publishing, 1993
La Mesa, CA
(619) 460-9030
$15, 368 pages

Other Trends in Alternative Medical Care

HOMEOPATHIC REBOUND Homeopathy was last embraced by large numbers of consumers at the turn of the century, and it is now enjoying a comeback. Originally created by Samuel Hahnemann, a German pharmacist, homeopathy is based on the concept that "like cures like." Diseases and ailments are treated with diluted amounts of the substances that cause the disease. For instance, poison ivy is used to treat poison ivy, and ipecac is used to treat nausea or vomiting. Because homeopathic medicines are typically diluted to a few parts per million, many physicians believe they are not harmful, but homeopathic cures have never been proven effective, at least not in the eyes of the medical establishment. Word-of-mouth testimony, however, is helping build a new following for this old concept. The major attraction for many is control of treatment, since homeopathy often can be practiced without the help of a professional. Adherents also appreciate homeopathy's link to the natural world, something most modern medicines seem to lack. Homeopathy has already attracted a large enough audience to convince some national drugstore chains to carry prepackaged homeopathic remedies.

RESOURCES:

Office of Alternative Medicine
National Institutes of Health
Bethesda, MD
(301) 594-7811
(new division of the National
Institutes of Health created to study
and report on alternative medical
practices)

International Foundation for
Homeopathy
Seattle, WA
(206) 324-8230
(national organization promoting
education, research, and treatment
with homeopathy)

MUSHROOM MEDICINE Mushrooms are gaining prominence as treatments for conditions ranging from inflammation to cancer. Their popularity appears to be an outgrowth of the "food as medicine" movement. Beneficial mushrooms include shiitake, reishi, and maitake, among others.

TIBETAN POINT HOLDING This practice is similar to acupressure. Two to five participants maintain contact with specific pressure points on the patient for up to two hours while the patient verbalizes particular emotional problems.

CHINESE REMEDIES Public support in the U.S. is strongly in favor of protecting endangered animal species such as the black rhinoceros. Some traditional Chinese remedies, however, use parts of endangered species as medical cures. A conflict could develop from this practice, as college-educated consumers seek more traditional Chinese drugs for ailments such as fading memory, loss of sexual function, and general aging.

RESOURCES:

American Foundation of Traditional
Chinese Medicine
San Francisco, CA
(415) 776-0502
(national organization involved
with education, research, and
treatment using traditional Chinese
medicines)

CRANIOSACRAL THERAPY This relatively new therapy was derived from research by an osteopath, or practitioner of pressure-based treatments, on the natural role of the dura mater, the membrane on the outer surface of the spinal cord and brain. This therapy uses light pressure to manipulate the dura mater, reportedly restoring a healthy "pulse" throughout the system. Practitioners believe an irregular or weak pulse in the dura mater is linked to conditions such as migraine headaches, back pain, and dyslexia.

RESOURCES:

The Upledger Institute
Palm Beach Gardens, FL
(407) 622-4334
(commercial facility providing
craniosacral therapy)

NAPRAPATHY Naprapathy employs manipulation of connective tissue to relieve pain. The treatment dates to the turn of the century, but it has only recently gained a measure of respectability because of a new state law in Illinois. The law recognizes the validity of the therapy and regulates the licensing of practitioners. The only center for training naprapaths in the U.S. is in Chicago.

RESOURCES:

Chicago National College of
Naprapathy
Chicago, IL
(312) 282-2686
(educational institution for training
naprapaths)

HEALTH AND
MEDICINE

NATURAL MENOPAUSE TREATMENTS Aging baby-boom women are bringing menopause to the forefront of women's medical issues and creating a niche market for alternative medicines that relieve the discomforts of menopause. Natural medicines, tonics, and dietary supplements marketed for nature-minded menopausal consumers include Chinese herbal concoctions (ginseng, dong quai, white peony, and licorice root, among others); acupuncture treatments; megadoses of vitamins, minerals, and amino acids; cleansing diets; and various massage and polarity therapies. Some supplement manufacturers are also taking advantage of the growing number of women who are reluctant to participate in estrogen-replacement therapy, which is commonly used to relieve the unpleasant symptoms of menopause. These companies are packaging various natural, herbal, and homeopathic alternative treatments.

RESOURCES:

The Menopause Self Help Book; A Women's Guide to Feeling Wonderful for the Second Half of Her Life
By Susan M. Lark
Celestial Arts, 1990
Berkeley, CA
(415) 524-1801
$16.95, 239 pages

SPECIALIZATION Practitioners of alternative therapies are increasingly specializing to market their services. Such approaches as meditation for divorce, holistic law, holistic dentistry, yoga psychology, and sexual healing combine alternative-care disciplines and focus attention on elementary problems.

RESOURCES:

International Association of
Holistic Health Practitioners
Las Vegas, NV
(702) 873-4542
(industry association for health care professionals using holistic methods)

Holistic Dental Association
Oklahoma City, OK
(405) 840-5600
(industry association for dentists using holistic methods)

MASSAGE MOVEMENTS More massage therapists are offering on-site services, traveling to offices, clinics, hospital rooms, home sickrooms, and sports clubs to give massages. Sports massage is also increasingly popular among both amateur and professional athletes. Specialists in sports massage—sometimes referred to as performance massage—concentrate on participants in specific sports and their unique physiological problems. Some massage therapists have developed practices specializing in trauma touching, the treatment of victims of trauma, violence, and sexual abuse using massage techniques. Massage therapy recently won the affirmation of the nursing community. The National Federation of Specialty Nursing Organizations has accepted the National Association of Nurse Massage Therapists into its ranks. The nurse massage therapists are now working to establish national certification standards for members of the organization.

RESOURCES:

International Sports Massage
Federation and Training Institute
Costa Mesa, CA
(714) 642-0735
(national organization involved in
education and training for sports
massage)

National Association of Nurse
Massage Therapists
Jupiter, FL
(407) 746-8860
(industry association for
professional nurses using
massage techniques)

Colorado School of Healing Arts
Lakewood, CO
(303) 986-2320
(educational facility involved with
therapeutic body work and trauma
touch therapy)

Kurashova Institute
Peoria, IL
(309) 786-4888
(educational facility involved with
Russian Sports massage)

INSURANCE ACCEPTABILITY Insurance companies have begun to include alternative treatments as reimbursable expenses for some kinds of health conditions, including accidents, pregnancy, and surgical recovery. Some have expanded coverage to include more esoteric treatments such as aromatherapy, shiatsu massage, Ayurvedic medicine (an ancient Indian system of diet and philosophy), guided imagery, and reflexology. But most mainstream companies will not pay for treatments beyond traditional massage therapy, acupuncture, and chiropractic care.

RESOURCES:

American Western Life Insurance
Company
Foster City, CA
(415) 573-8041
(health insurance underwriter)

Experienced Birthing

American interest in the European tradition of doulas is increasing. Doulas (from the Greek word meaning "helper") are assistants who traditionally help new mothers for the first few weeks after the birth of a child. The use of doulas also is expanding to assistance with children. In the European tradition, doulas were often relatives or older women with child-rearing experience. Today, doulas are more often professionals, whose practices are similar to those of midwives.

Doulas have been gaining respect and generating interest because of the positive results they achieve. The emotional and practical support they provide to new mothers helps them establish healthy bonds with their newborns and diminish the stress and disruption a new arrival brings to the family. Doulas are also used in maternity wards as friendly support for mothers and to mitigate the clinical atmosphere of hospitals. They are frequently matched with pregnant women to provide support and advice from mid-term through delivery.

Doulas have only recently become accepted by the American medical system, and they are not widely used in medical settings. There are programs to train and certify doulas, who may do anything from massage a pregnant woman to counsel her to relieve anxiety. Studies over the past decade have shown marked improvements in the birth process when doulas are involved. In one such study, the percentage of cesarean deliveries dropped from 18 percent to 8 percent in a group of pregnant women who were assigned doulas, compared with a control group. In another study, the average length of labor decreased from 19 hours to 9 hours.

In home settings, doulas provide useful information, advice, and guidance to mothers who may have had much less exposure to traditional mothering wisdom than women of previous generations. The result leads to calmer, more competent mothers, and healthier babies.

Some communities are borrowing practices of the doula tradition, especially those isolated from the support services usually found in major metropolitan areas. In these smaller communities, groups of volunteer women with child-rearing experience organize home visits to new mothers. This kind of grass-roots program with its simple advice and friendly support is credited with reducing the risk of family dysfunction, juvenile delinquency, and domestic and other acts of violence.

Doulas are expensive, which means the women and families who are most likely to benefit from their help probably can't afford them. They charge as much as $25 per hour. When they charge a flat fee for specified services, the average cost in the U.S. is $300. No insurance companies yet cover such services, although this may change within the next few years.

RESOURCES:

Mothering the Mother: How a Doula Can Help You Have a Shorter, Easier, and Healthier Birth
By Marshall H. Klaus, John H. Kennell, and Phyllis H. Klaus
Addison-Wesley, 1993
Reading, MA
(617) 944-3700
$19.95, 168 pages

National Association of Childbirth Assistants
San Jose, CA
(408) 225-9167
(industry association for personnel involved in assisting in childbirth)

Smart Drugs/Smart Politics

A serious and committed industry has established itself around a new class of drugs and nutrients known as "smart drugs." These drugs, a range of prescription and nonprescription products, include vitamins, amino acids, botanically derived compounds, and chemicals that promote neurological reactions.

One of the tools used to bring about acceptance of these substances is legitimate research conducted by mainstream medical groups around the world. Evidence linking aging, loss of cognitive facilities, loss of memory, and other debilitating mental states with irregular or missing chemical compounds in the brain is accumulating. The smart-drug industry has assembled data and guidelines from this research with which individuals can both protect against cognitive losses and possibly—controversy flares about this issue more so than other elements of this type of application of research findings—boost cognitive and memory functions in normal, unimpaired people. The problem: products are being promoted for specific cures and enhancing mental functions before the medical community has warranted such claims.

The difficulty for conservative medical practitioners is applying "fixes" to unbroken physical conditions. The function of the medical community is to fix what goes wrong, not improve on natural states of being. The conflict with the smart-drug industry could conclude within a few years with the much larger and more organized forces of the medical community—allied with the FDA—creating new restrictive rules about the kinds of drugs that can be sold for specific purposes. Within a year, the result may be new barriers for sales of amino acids and megadoses of vitamins, effectively removing them from general sale to the public through retail outlets.

One development aimed at adding more potential for applications of such substances is the attempt by some pharmaceutical companies and medical experts to establish a new category of disease: age-associated memory impairment (AAMI). Depression and post-traumatic stress syndrome are two examples of disorders that have become more "acceptable" by the medical industry after being officially categorized. AAMI would include a range of symptoms—memory loss, loss of alertness, lack of reasoning ability, etc.—and allow smart drugs to be prescribed as treatment. Because everybody ages, and virtually all aging past the age of 40 is accompanied by some degree of loss of mental ability, AAMI could become a major new social condition.

Currently, the strongest interest in anti-aging drugs related to mental conditions is focused on deprenyl, an MAO inhibitor used to treat Parkinson's disease, and melatonin, a naturally occurring hormone connected to circadian rhythms. (See "Field Effects," page 60.) There are as many as 150 drugs currently being studied in various countries for their potential in enhancing mental performance. Reports also exist of new underground chemistry research on the West Coast, where new variations of existing cognitive compounds are being explored by maverick chemists not content to wait for wider mainstream support in this country.

RESOURCES:

Jerry Emmanuelson
Colorado FutureScience
Colorado Springs, CO
(719) 634-0185
(research and consulting in smart
drugs)

Smart Drugs II: The Next Generation
by Ward Dean, John Morgenthaler,
and Steven Fowkes.
Health Freedom Publications, 1993
Millbrae, CA
(415) 583-9443
$14.95, 288 pages

*Brain Boosters: Foods and Drugs that
Make You Smarter*
by Beverly Potter and Sebastian
Orfali
Ronin Publishing, 1993
Berkeley, CA
(510) 540-6228
$12.95, 215 pages

SCIENCE AND COMPUTERS

SCIENCE AND COMPUTERS

Online will be the way to go for computer users in 1994, and providers of online services will be competing for their business. Computer makers will begin producing PCs with the most powerful microprocessor made to date, while scientists will be hard at work developing all kinds of products that are easier on the environment than their conventional counterparts.

Computer Trends

In 1993, chip manufacturers began unleashing a new generation of more powerful microchips. Led by Intel's Pentium, these faster microprocessors will provide desktop accessibility for image processing, multiuser capabilities, rapid multimedia functioning, voice processing, and large-scale database manipulation. The new chips will increase computer speed well beyond what is currently available in PCs. All of the new chips are expected to run at least at 100 millions of instructions per second (MIPS). Few of today's 486 chips operate at even half that rate. Commercial availability of only one such fast chip would create a significant new standard for personal computers, but within a few years, competing chips from several companies will result in lower prices for computer consumers.

Among the microprocessors that will compete with Pentium are:

■ **68060,** from Motorola, which will power Apple's Macintosh computers at up to three times their current speed.

■ **R4400,** from Silicon Graphics Technology, a Reduced Instruction Set Chip (RISC) for running graphics programs at up to 150 MHz, the fastest speed yet for personal computers. It will allow a wider range of program types to be used.

■ **PowerPC 601,** made by Motorola in cooperation with Apple and IBM, a 32-bit chip that is reportedly comparable in speed with the Pentium. It will be used in upcoming models of Macs and IBM PCs. Compatibility with earlier models will not be possible without special translation software.

■ **Alpha 21064,** from Digital Equipment, a 64-bit microprocessor that will run at speeds of 200 MHz. The Alpha is now being used in mini-computers, and Digital and Olivetti plan to use it in their new PCs.

■ **New 486s,** from Intel, Cyrix, and Advanced Micro Devices, which will run at up to 100 MHz.

■ **Pentium clones,** from Cyrix and Advanced Micro Devices, which will follow Pentium within 12 to 18 months of its introduction and perform almost as well as the original.

With the introduction of these new powerful microprocessors, current top-of-the line PC models, especially 486-based machines, will drop rapidly in price (likely by mid-1994), and 386-based units will become essentially obsolete. For all practical purposes, the 486-powered PCs may be obsolete also, because like most new computer technologies, the new chips will be incompatible with most existing software. Compatibility will depend on the chip. Intel's Pentium is thought to be the most versatile so far. Most major software companies plan to market versions of their programs that are compatible with Pentium. Windows NT, a new version of Microsoft's popular Windows program, is already Pentium-compatible.

Most 486-based machines will require expensive upgrades to the powerful Pentium microprocessor. The latest generation of 486 machines are being marketed as "Pentium upgradable," and although this is technically true, running these computers with add-on Pentium chips will not allow complete harnessing of the chips' internal speed or processing power. PCs with custom-designed electronic architecture are required for maximum performance of Pentium.

For many PC users, 1994 may mark the beginning of another "wait-and-see" period. Many will hold off on purchasing new equipment, while debating the value of upgrading recently purchased equipment. In 1994, prices for low-end PCs built with the new chips will be $2,500 to $2,900, which is about the cost of lower-priced 486 machines in 1993.

RESOURCES:

Intel Corporation
Santa Clara, CA
(408) 765-8080
(manufacturer of microprocessors)

Cyrix Corporation
Richardson, TX
(214) 994-8388
(manufacturer of microprocessors)

Advanced Micro Devices, Inc.
Sunnyvale, CA
(408) 732-2400
(manufacturer of microprocessors)

Silicon Graphics, Inc.
Mountainview, CA
(415) 960-1980
(manufacturer of microprocessors)

Digital Equipment Corporation
Maynard, MA
(508) 493-5111
(manufacturer of microprocessors)

Motorola, Inc. Microprocessor and
Memory Technology Group
(512) 891-2000
(manufacturer of microprocessors)

Other Computer Trends

DISTRIBUTED DATA STRUCTURES Companies are using the concept of distributed data structures (DDSs) to do away with more expensive mainframe computers. With a DDS, data and software programs are stored in PCs scattered throughout a company, in PCs in the same building, or in other locations. Data can even be stored in multiple locations in a local-area network (LAN) or wide-area network (WAN). A DDS essentially links the storage capacity of many PCs. PCs previously were not effective for storing large amounts of data because each PC could only allow a limited number of users to connect to it. To be effective, DDSs must have sophisticated sharing protocols that allow simultaneous data exchange among many users. Before they become widely used, the architects of DDSs must devise a way to separate general-access data from sensitive, secure data, and a way to back up individual PC sites within the DDS.

RESOURCES:

Sybase, Inc.
Emeryville, CA
(510) 596-3500
(development and publication of relational database-management software)

Transarc Corporation
Pittsburgh, PA
(412) 338-4400
(development and publication of Unix systems software)

CODED CONTROL Interest in encryption for computer data and programs is increasing. Actual use of encryption programs is difficult to track, but judging by the increasing amount of dialog on the subject, more individuals and companies are using coding as a way of protecting material. Encryption converts data into a coded format that cannot be read or deciphered by unauthorized users. Government interest in encryption is also increasing. Proposals from government bodies include plans to control nationwide wireless telephone technology to allow electronic eavesdropping only by government agents and to keep data files from being duplicated through the Internet.

Software companies working in the personal computer field are creating a wide variety of personal cryptographic controls for individuals to use. Shareware publishers—creators of low-cost programs that are distributed "free" in return for a promised payment if the programs are used—are getting in on the act also.

Telephone transmission encryption is likely to become a more significant issue for cellular-phone users as indications from the scanner industry—manufacturers of devices capable of receiving messages sent through police, fire, ambulance, airline, and other frequencies—point to widespread use of police-radio scanners to listen in on wireless telephone conversations. These readily available devices monitor radio calls and conversations by police and fire departments, and airplanes. Their circuitry is easily altered to allow eavesdropping on phone calls.

RESOURCES:

Scanners and Secret Frequencies
by Henry L. Eisenson
Index Publishing Group, 1993
San Diego, CA
(619) 281-2957
$19.95, 320 pages

CELLULAR DATA The wireless movement will continue to expand rapidly in the next few years, due to demand and the increasing availability of wireless technology that allows data to be transferred without telephone lines. By the end of 1993, McCaw Cellular Communications Company, recently acquired by AT&T and one of the nation's largest cellular-phone companies, is expected to initiate wireless service in half of the 105 cities in which it operates. By mid-1994, such services will be available in all cities. McCaw's system relies on a specification protocol known as Cellular Digital Packet Data (CDPD), with which digital signals are transmitted to and from cellular phones. CDPD has been adopted by at least seven cellular providers who will use the technology to provide services such as e-mail, database connections, electronic dispatching, and interactive messaging. (See also "Cellular Smart Phones," page 48.)

RESOURCES:

McCaw Cellular Communications
Company, Inc.
Kirkland, WA
(206) 827-4500
(cellular-telephone services)

PRICE TRENDS Driven by the arrival of a new generation of post-486 chips, prices for current personal-computer models should continue to drop in 1994. At mail-order retailers and discount outlets, prices for fast 486 units should drop below $1,500 and be priced as low as $1,000 by the end of the year. Macintosh prices, already discounted by Apple in a bid to stay competitive, should echo the PC trend, but Apple has less of a profit margin on Macs to give away as price concessions. Instead, look for Macs with added features, especially memory and speed.

RESOURCES:

Electronic Industries Association
Washington, DC
(202) 457-4900
(industry association of suppliers
and manufacturers of electronic
parts and equipment)

ONLINE HELP New Macs will reportedly be sold with all user warranty information and user support provided only through online connections. Users will be required to access the telecommunications features of their computers to go online with the service bureau at Apple. Once online, users will find additional information and entertainment sources, much of it provided by the Apple bulletin-board service. The company anticipates that these features will turn users into online fans.

RESOURCES:

Apple Computer, Inc.
Cupertino, CA
(408) 996-1010

(developer and manufacturer of
personal-computer hardware and
software)

Online Fare War

Many of the most popular online information services will cost users less in 1994. Beginning in 1993, competition and complaints from users were incentives for these services to lower their prices. Online services will not only reduce per-minute charges, but also offer more economical packages, such as flat rates for specified blocks of time.

Online services that cater to the general public, such as Prodigy, are facing an increasingly tenuous future. Factors limiting their growth include competition, market saturation, and inexpensive or free alternatives to many of their services. The latter may prove the most formidable foe. Users can now get information such as online encyclopedias, article abstracts, and company profiles from local services run by libraries, city governments, and "freenets." These public systems provide access to community information and additional resources to the general public at no charge. (The costs of operating these public systems are typically paid by cities and libraries.)

Systems such as the Cleveland Freenet, the PEN system in Santa Monica, California, and the Colorado Freenet are proliferating. The Cleveland system, dating back to 1986, now has more than 30,000 members and reports more than 10,000 connections to the network daily.

What makes these systems potent competition for fee-based services is information content, conferencing capabilities, and e-mail availability. These electronic services are often linked to public-library and academic-library databases, which provide a range of information, from encyclopedias, book reviews, entertainment schedules, weather reports, and magazine articles to local zoning codes and minutes of city-council meetings. Some freenets carry the text of tomes such as the Bible, the Koran, the Book of Mormon, and the U.S. Constitution.

A survey by *Online Access Magazine* in 1993 revealed there are at least 40 freenets under development and at least 12 already online. Other countries that are offering or planning to include similar services are Canada, Germany, Finland, Japan, and New Zealand. (Note: a list of some established commercial online services can be found in the Appendices, page 256.)

Another competitive factor facing many online services is the growing popularity of the Internet, a massive connection of networks and databases that is becoming easier to access. The Internet previously was the domain of academicians, but its use is becoming a trendy computer pastime. Books, software, and tutorials are proliferating, all with the goal of making this awkward system more palatable to the average user. At the same time, it has only been in the last two years that personal accounts on the Internet have become available through local, regional, and national organizations.

With its growing popularity, the Internet is headed for gridlock. At the current rate of increase in use, the Internet is projected to run out of usable e-mail addresses by 1995. Solutions to this problem are being discussed by the Internet Architecture Board, the organization responsible for decisions regarding how the Internet is set up and run. The most likely solution will involve the adoption of a new software protocol that permits more efficient utilization of addresses, in effect cramming more parts into a fixed amount of space. The current protocol is known as TCP/IP. (See also "E-mail Madness," page 26.)

One of the resources both experienced and novice users of the Internet are likely to welcome is a new service from AT&T, the Directory of Directories. This online listing includes most Internet sources and provides full-text searching of Internet users, organizations, and information sources.

RESOURCES:

Cleveland Freenet
Cleveland, OH
(216) 368-3888 (modem)
(public-information system)

Texas Internet Consulting
Austin, TX
(512) 451-6176
(computer network and Internet consulting)

AT&T InterNIC Directory and Database Service administrator
(908) 668-6587
InterNIC Information Services Referral Desk
(800) 444-4345
(AT&T Internet resources)

National Public Telecomputing Network
Cleveland, OH
(216) 247-5800
(national organization involved with publicly accessible networks)

Internet: Mailing Lists
by Edward Hardie and Vivian Neou
PTR Prentice Hall, 1993
Des Moines, IA
(515) 284-6751
$26, 368 pages

Internet Business Report
published by CMP Publications, Inc.
Manhasset, NY
(516) 562-5000
(Internet newsletter)

Library Resources on the Internet:
Strategies for Selection and Use
by Laine Farley and Mary Engle
American Library Association
Books Publishing Services, 1992
Chicago, IL
(800) 545-2433)
$20, 43 pages

Matrix News
published by Matrix Information
and Directory Services
Austin, TX
(512) 451-7602
(Internet newsletter)

SCIENCE AND
COMPUTERS

Data Highway Politics

Increasing publicity about the "data highway" of the future is being touted by the Clinton administration and Vice President Gore in particular. This data highway will be, in effect, a system of telecommunications paths—allowing high-speed transmissions of large amounts of data—crossing the country like the interstate highway system. While this acknowledgment of the value and necessity of such an electronic system is welcomed by many, fears are mounting in the computer industry that federal involvement in such a project will create more problems than it will solve.

Private industry generally is skeptical of government involvement in development of the data highway, largely because of the negative effects associated with government control of large projects in the past. "The government's principal goal is not to make the greatest information highway that can be built. It's to get re-elected," said Ryal Poppa, chairman of the data storage technologies firm Storage Technology Corporation in a 1993 speech at the University of Colorado College of Business Administration. "That means they place the goal of building this project within the structure of how to get re-elected."

Meanwhile, consortiums of private companies are proceeding on their own toward development of a data highway, even though the 1994 federal budget may include some funding for the project. Here are some of the private ventures that are underway:

■ **US West** is upgrading its network to carry video signals as well as traditional telephone traffic. By the end of 1994, at least 100,000 US West customers in some western states will be connected to these higher-capacity lines.

■ **Tele-Communications, Inc.,** the nation's largest cable-TV company, announced in 1993 that it would spend $2 billion over four years to link at least 250 municipalities with fiber-optic cable. With fiber optics, the company can expand cable programming up to 500 channels and also implement interactive information exchange.

■ **Time Warner, Inc.** will initiate service on its first data superhighway in 1994, in Orlando, Florida. The highway will link users to digitized libraries of movies, books, and magazines, and provide them with video-conferencing, picture phones and data-transport services.

RESOURCES:

US West
Denver, CO
(800) 879-4357
(telephone and data transmission services)

Tele-Communications Inc.
Englewood, CO
(303) 267-5500
(cable television services)

Time Warner Cable,
Full Service Network
Orlando, FL
(407) 660-5525
(cable television information and entertainment services

Electronic Archives

The concept of the truly paperless office may never be more than a concept. Despite vast improvements in electronic information handling, such as those provided by personal computers, e-mail, and other alternatives to printed pages, the amount of paper used in American offices continues to increase faster than the office population. According to some estimates, 92 billion paper documents and more than 300 billion photocopies are created each year. But there are some indications that this paper flood has peaked, particularly in large companies with efficient electronic data handling systems. The first stage in the other direction—reducing paper use—however, is more likely to be in the storage and handling of archival documents than replacing paper used in daily transactions. (See also "Bank Changes," page 21.)

Archiving has always presented a serious problem for businesses.

Storage space, record keeping, access, and preservation all must be addressed. At worst, many companies have faced serious economic difficulties in managing archival information. Computerization has long seemed to be the obvious answer, but the high cost and limited practicality of computer archival systems has hindered many businesses.

Help is on the way. Computer systems with mass storage capability and practical software for organizing records cost less than they did just a few years ago. High-speed, high-resolution scanning devices allow translation of paper-based images into electronic data at a minimum of cost and effort, but initial costs for these systems are high. The biggest applications in the near future for document imaging are in companies using local-area networks (LAN) and multiple work sites for entry and retrieval of information. From a few thousand users of LAN imaging systems in 1991, this field is expected to surpass 100,000 users by 1994.

Part of the challenge of replacing paper files with electronic archives is improving the search mechanism used to locate archived information. Simple keyword systems are all that is necessary to organize and retrieve documents. But many businesses need to search documents or images that are loosely related. New software uses what is known as "fuzzy searching," which recognizes text patterns and similarities in content and style.

At the forefront of this advanced searching development is "intelligent character recognition" (ICR). In most existing systems, paper documents are scanned into electronic storage systems, using optical character recognition (OCR) programs to identify characters and translate them into digital form. ICR takes OCR one step further. It extends character recognition from simple typewriter output to different kinds of typefaces, and even to handwriting. ICR is expected to be much more accurate than OCR, which misreads 1 percent to 10 percent of the characters scanned. Using word and phrase recognition, dictionary and thesaurus capabilities, and more accurate recognition capabilities, ICR could allow very high-speed automated scanning of paper documents, turning piles of files into rich lodes of mineable electronic information.

RESOURCES:

Excalibur Technologies Corporation
McLean, VA
(703) 790-2110
(development and publication of
computer software)

ViewStar Corporation
Emeryville, CA
(510) 652-7827
(development and publication of
document management software)

Business Council on the Reduction
of Paperwork
Washington, DC
(202) 393-4700
(national organization of businesses,
associations, and government
agencies involved with the redesign
of government forms)

Electronic Document Delivery:
Matching Technology to Requirement
Seybold Publications, 1993
Media, PA
(800) 325-3830
$24.95, 30 pages

Technology Trends

Significant impact on society from technological progress more often comes from innovation than invention. It may take several years to several decades for an invention—a technological breakthrough—to have commercial applications through gradual innovations. Technological innovations that will soon yield commercial results include the following:

WIND-SENSITIVE PAINT A new paint developed at the University of Washington glows in response to changes in air pressure. One potential use is in wind tunnels as a replacement for individual air-pressure sensors.

RESOURCES:

Professor James Callis
University of Washington
Chemistry Department
Seattle, WA
(206) 543-1610
(experimental paint research)

RIGID POLYMERS A new class of plastics called Poly-X materials has been invented. These plastics are rigid materials with self-reinforcing characteristics. Unlike high-strength plastic composites, they are inexpensive and can be molded like conventional plastics. Pilot production began in 1993, and commercial use is expected by 1994.

RESOURCES:

Maxdem, Inc.
San Dimas, CA
(909) 394-0644
(research and development
involving rigid-rod polymers)

TENT REPELLENT A new type of material for tents will do more than keep out the wind and rain; it also will repel insects. Expel, a water-repellent, flame-retardant, insect-repellent tent fabric has been patented by the Graniteville Company. The fabric contains Permethrin, a proven insecticide. The EPA has approved Expel for use as a tenting material; so it will initially show up on pop-up campers, hunting blinds, and boats. The company has applied to the EPA for approval of Expel for use next to animal and human skin. This would also make it a useful material for items such as horse blankets and outdoor clothing.

RESOURCES:

Graniteville Company
Graniteville, SC
(803) 663-2609
(manufacturer of specialty fabrics)

BUCKYBALL ADVANCES Buckminsterfullerene, or buckyballs, is a recently discovered type of carbon that is getting the attention of more potential users of the substance. The carbon atoms in Buckminsterfullerene are shaped like geodesic domes, making the material exceptionally small and light. In 1993, MicroMet Technology introduced the first buckyball product, a special steel known as Rhondite. The latest advances include the development of "buckytubes," and Bell Labs has also recently patented a buckyball product that converts light into electricity.

RESOURCES:

Bell Laboratories
Livingston, NJ
(908) 582-3000
(materials research and
development)

MicroMet Technology
Charlotte, NC
(704) 846-0522
(research and development in
buckminsterfullerenes)

SUPER WIRE Superconducting materials have been a laboratory curiosity for several years but have not made their way into the commercial world. These materials conduct electricity with little or no resistance, but they only work at extremely low temperatures, and they are too brittle for normal use in electrical wiring. A new less-brittle ceramic wire may make superconducting materials more practical for commercial users. It can be rolled, twisted, and manipulated.

RESOURCES:

American Superconductor
Corporation
Watertown, MA
(508) 836-4200
(research and development in
superconducting materials)

LASER MINING A new laser drilling technique has been devised that appears to be much more effective than earlier attempts to bring laser technology to the mining industry. A laser beam is projected through a stream of water at ore-bearing rock. The laser fractures the ore into small pieces, which are then washed away for refining. Advantages of this type of drilling include reduced use of explosives; carefully controlled, targeted ore extraction; decreased environmental damage; and reduced costs.

RESOURCES:

Interpro
Golden, CO
(303) 279-2581
(metallurgical research group)

HIGH-TECH CONVENTIONAL MICROSCOPES For decades, electron microscopes have been the most powerful available. Now new developments are making traditional optical microscopes much more powerful instruments. This technology is referred to as near-field scanning optical microscopes (NSOMs). Higher-resolution optical microscopes can be more practical than electron microscopes in some applications because a wider variety of viewing samples can be used.

RESOURCES:

Eric Betzig
AT&T Bell Labs
Marie Hill, NJ
(908) 582-3000
(technological research)

FLASH FREEZING A new concept in freezer technology can cut the time it takes to freeze a product from hours to minutes. This technology utilizes special liquids to remove heat from the products, while a special membrane separates the liquid from the products. Originally developed to freeze blood plasma and other protein-based substances without damaging them, the technology is also expected to be used by the food industry in the near future.

RESOURCES:

Instacool, Inc. of North America
Rancho Cordova, CA
(916) 638-8357
(manufacturer of ultra-rapid
chill/freezing equipment)

MORE MILITARY STEALTH Although the U.S. Air Force denies it, a new stealth aircraft may be patrolling the skies today. Civilian sources refer to the plane as the "Aurora" and believe it travels as fast as Mach 6, which is six times faster than the speed of sound. "Aurora" may already be in service for high-altitude spying. This high-tech aircraft is thought to be designed for higher altitudes than the Stealth bomber, but could be made from the same composite materials.

RESOURCES:

Aerospace America
published by American Institute of
Aeronautics and Astronautics, Inc.
Washington, DC
(202) 646-7471

1994 NASA LAUNCH SCHEDULE

Flight Mission	Date	Vehicle	Crew	Duration
62	1/94	Columbia	5	9 days

Payload: United States Microgravity Payload (USMP-02); Dextrous End Effector (DEE); Office of Aeronautics and Space Technology experiments (OAST-02)

63	3/94	Discovery	5	7 days

Payload: Lidar In-Space Technology Experiment (LITE I); Shuttle Pointed Autonomous Research Tool for Astronomy (SPTN-204); Robotic Materials Processing System (ROMPS-01)

64	5/94	Atlantis	6	7 days

Payload: Commercial pressurized experiment module (SPACEHAB- 03); Getaway Special Experiments (GAS BRIDGE); Shuttle Pallet Satellite— Infrared Background Survey (SPAS-III); International Extreme-Ultraviolet Far-Ultraviolet Hitchhiker (IEH-01); Real Time Environmental and Agricultural Monitoring (RTEAM)

65	6/94	Endeavor	7	9 days

Payload: Cryogenic Infrared Spectrometer Telescope for Atmosphere (CRISTA-SPAS); Atmospheric Laboratory for Applications and Science (ATLAS-03); Shuttle Solar Backscatter Ultra-Violet Instrument (SSBUV-A-03)

66	7/94	Columbia	7	13 days

Payload: International Microgravity Laboratory (IML-02)

67	9/94	Discovery	7	7 days

Payload: Ultraviolet Telescope (ASTRO-02); Shuttle Pointed Autonomous Research Tool for Astronomy (SPTN-201-02); Extended Duration Space Environment Candidate Materials Exposure (CMSE-01)

Additional NASA launch events for 1994 include:

Date	Rocket	Launch Site
5/94	Delta II	Vandenberg AFB (CA)

Payload: Polar Auroral Plasma Physics satellite (POLAR)

| 5/94 | Delta II | Vandenberg AFB (CA) |

Payload: Laser Geodynamics Satellite (LAGEOS III)

| 9/94 | Pegasus | Wallops Flight Facility (VA) |

Payload: Fast Auroral Snapshot Explorer (FAST)

| 12/94 | Atlas I | Cape Canaveral Air Force Station (FL) |

Payload: Geostationary Operational Environmental Satellite (GOES-J)

| 12/94 | Delta II | Vandenberg AFB (CA) |

Payload: Radar Satellite (RADARSAT)

| 12/94 | Pegasus | Wallops Flight Facility (VA) |

Payload: Satellite de Aplicaciones Cientificas—Argentine spectrometer satellite (SAC-B); High Energy Transient Experiment (HETE)

Source: NASA Space Shuttle Operations Office, Houston, TX; (713) 483-6246. This information is also available online on the NASA BBS, (205) 895-0028.

Environmental Trends

FRIENDLY BACTERIA The use of specialized bacteria—some natural, some bioengineered—to consume unwanted materials is now a widespread commercial practice. Bacteria are used to attack oil spills, consume contaminated garbage, and eat leftover grease from food products. Human blood, a substance now requiring careful disposal because of the risk of contamination from various diseases, including AIDS, soon may be disposed of by hungry bacteria. Envirogen is making progress in developing bacteria that can degrade some hydrochlorofluorocarbons (HCFCs). The organisms tested so far are found naturally in the soil.

RESOURCES:

Envirogen, Inc.
Lawrenceville, NJ
(609) 936-9300
(research and development of
hazardous-waste treatments)

SOLVENT REPLACEMENTS Many industries are finding replacements for volatile solvents. Water-based paints and finishes have become commonly available for use in home remodeling, many printers are reducing plant emissions by switching to soy-based printing inks, propellants and solvents in hairsprays are being replaced, and most car makers are switching to water-born, base-coat paints or powder coatings. One common product that is quietly undergoing such a switch is correction fluid for typists. The Gillette Company, manufacturers of Liquid Paper, no longer makes this product with the traditional formula. It now uses a chemical called cyclohexane instead of solvents that deplete ozone in the atmosphere.

RESOURCES:

Gillette Stationery Products Group
Boston, MA
(617) 421-7000
(manufacturer of office products)

Cosmetic, Toiletry and Fragrance
Association
Washington, DC
(202) 331-1770
(industry association of suppliers,
manufacturers, and distributors of
cosmetics, fragrances, and personal-
care products)

Chemical Specialties
Manufacturers Association
Washington, DC
(202) 872-8110
(industry association of suppliers,
manufacturers, and marketers of
household and industrial chemical
products)

SRI International
Menlo Park, CA
(415) 326-6200
(market research and consulting)

CONTAMINATED PORTS Sediments found at the bottom of most ports in the U.S. are now believed to be contaminated with a variety of toxic materials, from dioxin to heavy metals. Dredging—once a routine process for maintaining the depth of shipping channels and expanding usable waterways—is now entering a new era of controls because of the fear of stirring up these toxins. Trends developing from this concern will include new government regulations and restrictions, delays in dredging in many ports, expanded research on the effects of dislodged toxins, and development of alternative disposal methods for dredged materials. Most sludge is now dumped in off-shore sites.

RESOURCES:

Environmental Action Foundation
Takoma Park, MD
(301) 891-1100
(national organization involved with
research and education in energy
policy, toxic waste, and waste-
reduction programs)

BATTERY ALTERNATIVES In a consumer society increasingly plugged into battery-operated devices—most recently, portable computers, cellular telephones, and portable video games—the environmental hazards posed by batteries are not welcome news. In response to concerns about the negative effects of mercury and other toxic material found in most batteries, new battery types are being developed to reduce or remove the offending materials.

A more significant trend, however, is improvement in rechargeable batteries that may make rechargeables a permanent replacement for disposable batteries. In 1992, rechargeable batteries were in about 25 percent of U.S. homes, up from 14 percent in 1991. According to industry projections, sales of rechargeable batteries should increase at least 10 percent each year for the next three years. This growth will be due to a number of factors, including lower prices, more devices that use rechargeable batteries, and improved performance—quicker recharging time and longer use between recharges. New technology for rechargeable batteries will soon include a new nickel-metal-hydride unit to replace the current nickel-cadmium standard. The first nickel-metal-hydride rechargeable batteries are expected to hit the market in late 1993 or early 1994 and will offer marked improvements in performance.

Powered devices that use built-in rechargeable batteries are also the focus of a trend. More states, following the lead of Connecticut, Minnesota, and Vermont, are expected to enact legislation requiring manufacturers of such devices to design the battery packs so they can be removed when the devices are eventually thrown away.

RESOURCES:

Environmental Protection Agency
(202) 260-2090
(government agency involved with
environmental issues)

BLEACHING ALTERNATIVES With the paper recycling movement well underway, attention is now shifting to the problem of treating virgin and recycled paper pulp to make it whiter. The conventional method for bleaching paper is the use of chlorine-intensive chemicals. But because this method produces dioxin, an environmental contaminant, the process is increasingly under attack. Alternatives include the use of hydrogen-peroxide brighteners—a process gaining favor in Europe and already adopted by at least one paper supplier in the U.S., Lyons Falls Pulp & Paper—and reducing the amount of chlorine used.

Terminology in the paper industry is also changing to reflect this trend. New terms include Recycled Chlorine Free (RCF), which designates virgin fiber with no chlorine and recycled fiber without additional chlorine added; Total Chlorine Free (TCF), which applies to virgin fiber without chlorine; Secondarily Chlorine Free (SCF), another term for recycled fiber without additional chlorine; and Elemental Chlorine Free (ECF), which means the product is made from virgin fiber with chlorine derivatives but no chlorine.

RESOURCES:

Technical Association of the Pulp
and Paper Industry
Atlanta, GA
(404) 446-1400
(industry association of executives,
engineers, and researchers working
with paper, paper pulp, and
packaging)

Lyons Falls Pulp & Paper, Inc.
Lyons Falls, NY
(315) 348-8411
(manufacturer of paper products)

Industrial Recycling

CARPETS The Partnership for Carpet Reclamation, formed by a network of carpet manufacturing companies, began collecting and disposing of discarded carpeting in 1993. Used carpets are shredded in a central processing plant, after which they are tested for use as carpet cushioning and reinforcing material for asphalt and plastics.

RESOURCES:

Carpet and Rug Institute
Dalton, GA
(706) 278-3176
(industry association of suppliers and
manufacturers of carpets and rugs)

FLUORESCENT LAMPS The disposal of old fluorescent lamps is a growing environmental issue because of the presence of mercury in the bulbs. Many states have strict regulations on dumping fluorescent lamps in landfills, although some lamps have little or no mercury in them. The current trends in disposal: increasing state regulations requiring testing of spent lamps to determine toxicity, and additional fees for disposal.

RESOURCES:

National Lighting Bureau
Washington, DC
(202) 457-8437
(industry association of companies
and trade groups involved with
lighting products)

NYLON The Du Pont Company has reported progress in the development of new processes to recycle used nylon. Expectations are that up to 85 percent of all nylon in use today could be handled with the new processes, returning this polymer to the manufacturing end in a form clean enough to replace new nylon. Testing is now underway at a pilot nylon-recycling plant in Glasgow, Delaware.

RESOURCES:

E.I. du Pont de Nemours &
Company, Inc.
Wilmington, DE
(302) 774-1000
(manufacturer of petroleum-based
products)

LEAD The cost of removing and disposing of toxic lead-based paint when repainting bridges and other industrial structures is severely crimping repainting plans of many cities and states. One solution may be a new mobile lead-removal unit developed by Westinghouse Electric. The unit processes paint and sand-blasting debris on the site of the painting at a rate of two to four tons per hour and reduces lead content in the debris enough to cut disposal costs by as much as two-thirds.

RESOURCES:

The Environmental Group
Westinghouse Electric Corporation
Science and Technology Center
(412) 937-4066
(lead-paint disposal)

TIRES Rubber recycled from discarded automobile tires is gradually being accepted as a useful product by several industries. This coarsely ground material, or crumb rubber, is being used to add drainage and shock absorbency to lawns and athletic fields.

RESOURCES:

JaiTire
Denver, CO
(303) 322-7887
(supplier of recycled rubber-tire material)

Auto Emissions

The Environmental Protection Agency will require new 1994 passenger cars and light trucks to include internal monitoring devices to diagnose emissions. At the same time, a new generation of catalytic converters will make for cleaner auto emissions at a lower cost. Several companies, including AlliedSignal, Nissan Motor Company, and Ford Motor Company, have developed catalyst systems that do not require platinum or rhodium but use palladium instead.

The performance-car market is also changing to meet emissions requirements. "Green" engine components for hot-rod vehicles are one of the strongest growth areas in the automotive aftermarket, which is the market for parts and accessories bought after a vehicle is purchased. Included are exhaust components, turbochargers and superchargers, computer chips, valve-train parts, and electrical system components. These parts are part of an industry program that sets standards meeting or exceeding emissions requirements in all 50 states.

RESOURCES:

AlliedSignal, Inc.
Morristown, NJ
(201) 455-2000
(manufacturer of automotive products)

Nissan North America, Inc.
Detroit, MI
(313) 393-1893
(manufacturer of automotive products)

Performance and Specialty
Automotive News
published by SEMA Publications
Diamond Bar, CA
(909) 860-2961
(industry publication)

Ford Motor Company
Detroit, MI
(313) 322-3000
(manufacturer of automotive
products)

FOUR

THE CONSUMER

THE CONSUMER

When it comes to food in 1994, consumers will find more fat-laden fast food, along with new artificial sweeteners and fat-free products made with tastier fat replacers. Superstores selling everything from home electronics to pet food will dominate shopping in many markets, but consumers aren't completely sold. Many will make their way back to more convenient, smaller retailers.

Eating and Drinking in '94

Despite years of widespread concern over the fat content of food, Americans are eating more fat than ever. Consumption of fat will likely surpass 18 billion pounds in 1994, up from 14.4 billion pounds in 1990. At an annual increase of 6 percent a year, consumers' craving for fat is increasing faster than the population. The most popular fat is soybean oil. It accounts for about 13 billion pounds of the total fat consumed each year. About 75 percent of this goes into salad mixes.

At the same time, grocers' shelves are exhibiting an ever-growing number of fat-free products made with fat substitutes. Even though fat substitutes are still in the early stages of development, their sales already total $100 million a year. No single product has emerged as the dominant fat replacer, but one trend is developing: the creation of specific replacements for fats and oils in single food categories, such as frozen foods or salad dressings. Fat replacers that should be on the market soon include Nutricol konjac flour from Avicel; Oatrim from Rhone-Poulence and Quaker Oats; ConAgra Specialty Grain Products; new forms of Veri-Lo from Pfizer; new forms of Stellar from Staley; and Olestra, a sucrose polyester substance from Procter & Gamble. FDA approval for Olestra is pending. P&G's patent on Olestra will expire in 1994.

RESOURCES:

FMC Corporation Food and
Pharmaceutical Products Division
Philadelphia, PA
(215) 299-6000
(food-ingredients research and
development; Avicel)

Arthur D. Little, Inc.
Cambridge, MA
(617) 864-5770
(food-technology consulting)

ConAgra Specialty Grain Products
Omaha, NE
(402) 595-4000
(grain products, Oatrim fat
substitute)

Pfizer, Inc. Food Science Group
New York, NY
(212) 573-2323
(Veri-lo fat substitute)

A.E. Staley Manufacturing
Company
Decatur, IL
(217) 423-4411
(processed corn products, Stellar fat
substitute)

Procter & Gamble Company
Cincinnati, OH
(513) 983-1100
(Olestra fat substitute)

Dining Out

When economic times are tough, some consumers seek positive experiences to bolster their spirits. For the dining industry, that means increased sales of traditional American steak dinners, particularly at the top end of the market.

While consumption of red meat at home has declined from about 70 pounds per person a year in 1984 to about 60 pounds today—restaurants increasingly serve as a "counter-indulgence" for diners weary of watching their budgets, calories, and cholesterol. One of the largest upscale-restaurant chains known for its steak entrees is Morton's, which has 20 outlets across the country. Another 9 outlets are planned within the next year. Upscale establishments like Morton's provide large servings and a variety of traditional beef cuts. One mid-scale steak house chain is Outback Restaurants, first opened in 1987. By the end of 1993, the company expects to have 100 outlets.

Mainstream restaurants catering to families, however, are not yet part of this trend. For the mass market, even when dining out, nutrition and value are still a bigger draw. Within a few years, as with most trends in the restaurant industry, the focus on gourmet steak dinners will begin to affect the middle class and the mass market with lower-priced variations.

Value-awareness is one reason all-you-can-eat buffets are showing up in more locations. Some established chains are trying this format, including Pizza Hut, McDonald's, and KFC, all of which introduced all-you-can-eat restaurants in 1992. Most all-you-can-eat restaurants charge less than $10 for their buffets, but some new buffets are going after more upscale diners with prices in the $10-to-$20 range.

Following decades of growth for pizza, hamburger, and chicken fast-food restaurants, Asian cuisine eateries are coming on strong. Restaurant industry figures indicate that business at Asian fast-food outlets is increasing by 20 percent a year. Eighty percent of the growth in Asian fast food is attributable to Chinese restaurants, but Korean, Japanese, and Vietnamese cuisines are also gaining popularity. The largest players in Asian fast food are the Chinese chains Manchu Wok, China Bell, and Panda Express. Fast-food Asian outlets hope to fill the niche for convenient food not filled by the standard sit-down, mid-scale Asian restaurants that are typical in the U.S. Customers for these new eateries are expected to be middle-class consumers, eager for more fast-food variety and low-fat food made with fresh ingredients.

RESOURCES:

Technomic, Inc.
Chicago, IL
(312) 876-0004
(restaurant industry market research)

Morton's of Chicago, Inc.
Chicago, IL
(312) 923-0030
(steak restaurants)

Outback Steakhouse, Inc.
Tampa, FL
(813) 282-1225
(steak restaurants)

National Restaurant Association
Washington, DC
(202) 331-5900
(industry association of restaurants and other food-service companies)

Pizza Hut, Inc.
Wichita, KS
(316) 681-9000
(pizza restaurants)

McDonald's Corporation
Oak Brook, IL
(708) 575-3000
(hamburger restaurants)

KFC Corporation
Louisville, KY
(502) 456-8300
(fried-chicken restaurants)

Scott's Hospitality (Manchu Wok)
Toronto, Canada
(416) 369-9050
(Asian fast food)

Hix Nix Lean Cuisine

Sensing consumer interest in reduced-fat eating in recent years, the nation's fast-food restaurants have introduced a number of healthy alternatives to their typical fat-laden fare. But now many have lost heart. Innovations over the past few years, including the McLean Deluxe—McDonald's low-fat replacement for the all-American hamburger—have not fared well. Salad bars and diet colas notwithstanding, the current trend in fast-food eateries is more calories, not less. Offerings at fast-food outlets include more bacon, cheese, meat, and fat-saturated sauces. Consumers' fast-food choices are increasingly based on flavor, substance, fulfillment, and all-out indulgence. This return-to-basics attitude of fast-food chains is less an abrupt about-face and more a realization of what the masses want. Still, salad bars are so widely accepted by consumers that they are likely to remain fixtures at fast-food restaurants.

Although some consumers still make diet-conscious choices at the fast-food counter, many adults cease dieting or abiding by nutritional concerns as they close in on middle age. If they haven't achieved their desired body images by their mid-40s, it is more likely that they will abandon such attempts in subsequent years. While images of lean, well-exercised professionals proliferate on television and the covers of *Time* and *Newsweek,* the average American has more likely been maintaining a diet of fast food and watching television instead of exercising. Low-fat "heart-wise" cuisine will largely be the domain of sit-down restaurants and the choice of a minority of consumers.

Meanwhile, today's lighter groceries have also been struggling. Many introductions of these "light" products have failed or may soon do so. Among the casualties are snack foods, pancake syrups, and soups.

The failure to thrive in what was supposed to be a boom market for healthy foods is being blamed on several factors. One of them is that virtually all of the failed products were reformulated recipes attempting to create or recreate familiar tastes with substitute ingredients. Because of the unique taste characteristics and so-called "mouth feel" of natural fat, taste suffers when fat is removed or replaced. So far, fat substitutes just do not duplicate the taste of natural fat. Reduced-fat products have also been troubled by consumer confusion between familiar products and their "light" counterparts.

In spite of consumer rejection of many low-fat products, the light-food movement is not being abandoned completely. Reevaluation of the market is underway among the major food packagers. In the next few years, there are likely to be fewer new light versions of existing products; more carefully formulated light recipes that taste good, even if some fat must be added; and marketing campaigns to improve the image of light products. Finally, progress is being reported in the development of tastier fake fats.

RESOURCES:

Nutrition Education Association
Houston, TX
(713) 665-2946
(industry association of health professions working with nutrition and diet)

Dietetic Association
Chicago, IL
(312) 899-0040
(industry association of registered dietitians)

THE CONSUMER

Ersatz Update

Following the expiration of its aspartame patent in 1992, NutraSweet has been working on new forms of artificial sweeteners. One of these, Sweetener 2000, is 50 times as sweet as aspartame, which itself is 200 times as sweet as sugar. This new product should be available for commercial use in the year 2000. Johnson & Johnson's new sweetener, sucralose, should be introduced sooner than that. This sweetener is 600 times sweeter than sugar. Sucralose, whose trade name is Splenda, is already sold in Canada.

Trehalose is a sweetener derived from yeast that is now patented in the U.S. and Europe, and it also has food-preservation qualities. Vegetables, fruits, and meats can be dried with this product, giving them much longer shelf-life. When water is added, the trehalose helps the food maintain its original flavor, nutritional content, and texture. Other sugar substitutes under review by the FDA include alitame from Pfizer, and cyclamate from Abbott Laboratories.

Meanwhile, most major food and beverage manufacturers who use aspartame plan to continue using it. Developments in the diet-cola market, however, may eat away at the sweetener's dominance. Makers of light colas are reportedly creating hybrid diet drinks by adding small amounts of natural sugar to improve flavor. Diet colas with aspartame have only a few calories. The hybrid drinks would have about 30 calories. Regular sugar-sweetened colas have about 140 calories.

Pepsi is the first major beverage producer to embrace the emerging trend of "blended sweeteners." It is experimenting with a new diet cola sweetened with a combination of aspartame and a new artificial sweetener known as acesulfame-K. The new cola, called Pepsi Max, was introduced in Italy and the United Kingdom in 1993. Acesulfame-K is not yet approved for sale in the U.S. in bottled beverages, although it can be used in powdered drink mixes such as instant coffee. Similar soft drinks should appear in the U.S. as the FDA approves new sweeteners. The result should be better taste for consumers and cost savings of 30 percent to 40 percent for the producer.

RESOURCES:

Pfizer, Inc. Food Science Group
New York, NY
(212) 573-2323
(manufacturer of alitame)

Abbott Laboratories
Abbott Park, IL
(708) 937-6100
(manufacturer of cyclamate)

Osmotica Foods, Inc.
Sacramento, CA
(916) 753-6313
(joint venture of Calgene, Inc., and Quadrant Research to manufacture trehalose)

Calorie Control Council
Atlanta, GA
(404) 252-3663
(industry association of manufacturers of diet foods and beverages)

Pepsi Company, Inc.
Purchase, NY
(914) 253-2000
(manufacturer of soft drinks)

Hoechst Celanese Corporation
Somerville, NJ
(908) 231-2000
(manufacturer of acesulfame-K)

Johnson & Johnson
New Brunswick, NJ
(908) 524-1900
(manufacturer of sucralose)

Institute of Food Technologists
Chicago, IL
(312) 782-8424
(industry association of scientists researching food products, ingredients, and nutrition)

Cheaper Eats

Developers of artificial sweeteners aren't the only businesses in the food industry that are locked in intense competition. The current marketing battles among grocery chains, warehouse food outlets, and major food packagers are unlikely to ebb in 1994. Intensified competition is the more likely trend, with the result being lower food prices.

One battle is between packagers of brand-name products and those that package store brands. The arena is the grocery store, and major grocery chains are heating up the competition by developing more private-label products to compete with the big-name brands. Sales of private-label products in grocery stores are increasing by more than 3 percent a year and may reach $7 billion in 1994. In 1992, more than 18 percent of all grocery-store sales were generated by private-label products.

Brand-name packagers will counter this threat with reduced prices, additional promotions and advertising, rebates, coupons, and special displays. Some major manufacturers will adopt these tactics preemptively to discourage the introduction of competing private-label products. In addition, new-product development is expected to be used as a weapon. Brand-name companies typically have much larger budgets for creating new products than do their private-label competitors. Brand-name producers like Ralston Purina and Borden are even trying to beat private-label competitors at their own game by manufacturing their own brandless products.

Nonfood products are also scoring successes for private-label producers. Major growth is being reported for such items as plastic garbage bags, disposable diapers, laundry detergent, cigarettes, mouthwash, nonprescription pain killers, and disposable paper products.

Where is this consumer demand for private labels coming from? Some industry analysts interpret the demand as a cultural shift away from the excesses of the 1980s. More pragmatic observers point to the long-term trend of increasing middle-class and upscale consumer interest in private-label products, driven by a belief that those products are high in value, the combination of quality and affordability. This theme has been heard more and more often in many grocery stores since the 1970s. More recently, poor regional and national economic conditions are convincing more consumers to opt for value.

Low-income consumers, who have always preferred brand names

THE CONSUMER

to private labels, are still reluctant to snap up less-expensive brandless products. Brand-name packagers will be watching to see if they lose any of these customers to private labels. Consumers in all income categories may begin shifting back to brand-name products as economic conditions improve. The "value revolution" is not likely to become a permanent shopping habit.

In the meantime, consumers will get more price breaks on both name-brand and private-label products, as producers duke it out. In the end, added effort and promotion on the part of brand-name manufacturers may mean they will capture more attention and consumer dollars in coming years.

RESOURCES:

Ralston Purina Company
St. Louis, MO
(314) 982-1000
(manufacturer of cereals and
baked goods)

Borden, Inc.
New York, NY
(212) 573-4000
(manufacturer of dairy products
and snacks)

Private Label Manufacturers
Association
New York, NY
(212) 972-3131
(industry association of suppliers,
manufacturers, wholesalers,
retailers, and consultants working
with store brands)

Information Resources, Inc.
Chicago, IL
(312) 726-1221
(market evaluation)

Other Food Trends

NEW LABELING The Food and Drug Administration's new labeling standards take effect in May 1994. After that, most food-products manufacturers and packagers will be required to list more complete nutritional and ingredient information on package labels.

The new labels must include information on total calories, calories derived from fat, total fat, saturated fat, sodium, total carbohydrates, cholesterol, dietary fiber, sugars, protein, calcium, iron, and vitamins A and C. In addition, total grams for individual nutrients must be listed, as well as the percentage of recommended daily nutritional requirements.

These new label standards are unlikely to have much effect on sales.

Consumers respond more strongly to marketing slogans touting less cholseterol or no salt than to changes in the small print on the labels.

RESOURCES:

Food & Drug Administration
Center for Food Safety and
Applied Nutrition
Rockville, MD
(301) 443-1544
(government agency conducting
research and developing standards
for food, additives, and nutrition)

National Food Processors
Association
Washington, DC
(202) 639-5900
(industry association of commercial
food-product processors and
manufacturers)

FOOD ZAPPING Irradiated food, long dreaded by consumer-advocacy groups, has made its initial appearance into the nation's food system. Following recent government approval for the sale of irradiated fruits and vegetables, a limited number of food outlets has been selling such produce with generally favorable sales results. Irradiation kills microorganisms that cause produce to spoil. Treated products can gain weeks of usable shelf life. In 1994, the FDA is expected to approve irradiation for the processing of meat. Other food treatment methods being developed include pulsed-power technology, which uses short bursts of electrical energy to kill bacteria in bread, liquids, and other foods, and irradiating techniques that use electron beams or X rays instead of gamma rays, the type of radiation associated with irradiation.

RESOURCES:

American Meat Institute
Washington, DC
(703) 841-2400
(industry association of meat
packers, processors, and suppliers)

Vindicator, Inc.
Plant City, FL
(813) 752-3364
(gamma irradiation equipment)

Foodco Corporation
San Diego, CA
(619) 496-4100
(irradiation equipment)

FDA Center for Food Safety and
Applied Nutrition
Rockville, MD
(301) 443-1544
(government industry involved with
regulating irradiation technology)

Institute of Food Technologists
Chicago, IL
(312) 782-8424
(industry association of scientists
researching food products,
ingredients, and nutrition)

THE CONSUMER

KOSHER CACHET Sales of kosher foods are increasing, a trend related more to consumer interest in healthy, nutritious food with no additives than compliance with traditional Jewish customs. Kosher food sales are estimated at more than $32 billion a year, with an annual growth of 15 percent. One of the biggest potential growth areas within this market segment may be for kosher meats. Kosher certification requires that animals be raised without growth-stimulating chemicals.

RESOURCES:

Kosher Certification Service,
Union of Orthodox Jewish
Congregations of America
New York, NY
(212) 563-4000
(religious organization responsible
for Kosher food standards)

SALSA VARIATIONS With spicy sauces and condiments growing ever-more popular, competition and demand are inevitably producing changes. One of the newest changes is the marketing of fresh salsas in delis and refrigerated cases at supermarkets as an alternative to bottled varieties. Upscale home gourmets will also create more of their own sauces, a home-cuisine trend that will be accompanied by increasing sales of books, videotapes, ingredients, and even seeds for growing obscure kinds of hot peppers. Businesses will respond to salsa-mania with specialty products bottled by individual restaurants; premium, expensive salsas and hot sauces; chutneys and fruit-based salsas; and more salsas and hot sauces in fast-food outlets such as McDonald's and Wendy's.

RESOURCES:

Progressive Grocer
published by Progressive Grocer
Company
Stamford, CT
(203) 325-3500

LIGHT PIZZA Frozen pizza, already the number-one frozen food, should experience some increase in sales in the next few years as more manufacturers offer low-fat varieties. Frozen-pizza sales total $1.3 billion a year and are increasing at more than 3 percent annually. Tombstone Pizza, Healthy Choice, and Stouffer's Lean Cuisine already market light-pizza products. Most fans of frozen pizza, however, are not expected to alter their indulgences and opt for reduced-fat pizzas. The biggest concerns of frozen-pizza customers are price and taste, not calorie content.

RESOURCES:

National Frozen Pizza Institute
McLean, VA
(703) 821-0770
(industry association of manufacturers and suppliers of frozen-pizza products)

Stouffer Foods Corporation
Solon, OH
(216) 248-3600
(prepared frozen-foods manufacturer)

Tombstone Pizza Corporation
Northfield, IL
(708) 646-6000
(frozen-pizza manufacturer)

ConAgra Consumer Frozen Food Company
Omaha, NE
(402) 595-6000
(prepared frozen-foods manufacturer)

REMEDY FOODS Sales of "nutriceuticals," "health functional foods," or "prescriptive foods" are on the rise. These products are being touted as health-enhancing sources of energy and prevention. Prescriptive foods, which are most popular among natural-foods devotees, include vitamins and supplements as well as natural and organic products. Buoyed by recent reports of the health benefits of vitamins C, B, and E, among others, this food category is rapidly gaining support among middle- and upper-middle-class consumers with college educations, the consumers who are most likely to be concerned about aging and the effects of environmental factors on health. Among the offerings soon to be on store shelves are shiitake mushroom extract, a traditional tonic in Japan, and green tea, recently found to control tumor growth.

RESOURCES:

Prevention
published by Rodale Press, Inc.
Emmaus, PA
(215) 967-5171

CANNED BEANS Partly fueled by recent consumer concerns about the cost of food, sales of always-economical canned beans have been increasing nationwide. In addition, new federal guidelines about fiber and nutritional content of food have made beans a favorite of nutrition-conscious consumers, and they are more convenient than dried beans. Taking advantage of this new-found popularity, manufacturers of canned-bean products are adding new varieties, including those already in regional or test markets. Canned-bean trends include red lentils, canary beans, pinquinto beans, black beans, pink beans, and marinated and mixed beans for salads.

RESOURCES:

Goya Foods, Inc.
Secaucus, NJ
(201) 348-4900
(canned specialty-food products)

S&W Fine Foods, Inc.
San Ramon, CA
(510) 866-4500
(canned vegetables)

Del Monte Foods
San Francisco, CA
(415) 247-3000
(canned vegetables)

Vending-Machine Trends

Grocery stores aren't the only places that will be displaying new food stuffs in 1994. Consumers will also see new twists in food-dispensing vending machines. Innovations in the vending-machine industry have been slow to arrive in the U.S. Other countries, particularly Japan, have a major lead in the number and variety of vended products available. The most often cited reason U.S. consumers can only draw the ordinary from vending machines is the lack of a dollar coin.

The absence of a dollar coin in the U.S. currency system is being aggressively attacked in Washington, D.C., by vending-industry lobbyists and coin collectors. Those advocates, combined with some within the U.S. Treasury who support the introduction of a dollar coin, may trigger a change in policy within the next two years. While waiting for the dollar-coin problem to be resolved, new currency readers and credit-card and bank debit-card scanners have given vending-machine developers some flexibility.

GOURMET COFFEE Upscale coffee, which is already growing in popularity, may soon be available from vending machines. These may include espresso dispensers and coffee makers that grind fresh beans for each cup.

FROZEN FOODS The next generation of vending machines will be able to thaw and cook frozen foods in 30 seconds or less. These machines should be a boon to the sluggish vending-machine industry. The new machines store frozen foods at near 0 degrees Fahrenheit, which is comparable to many freezers. Vending interests are likely to market items such as breakfast snacks, pizza, pastries, and name-brand products like sandwiches from McDonald's and Burger King. Tests of frozen vended food have been underway in Florida since mid-1992, with promising results.

FRENCH FRIES Machine-dispensed french fries have failed in the past, but at least one new vending machine successfully produces fresh-cooked french fries.

RESOURCES:

Vending Times
published by Vending Times, Inc.
New York, NY
(212) 714-0101
(industry publication)

Ore-Ida Foods
Boise, ID
(208) 383-6100
(vending-machine french fries)

National Automatic Merchandising
Association
Chicago, IL
(312) 346-0370
(industry association of
manufacturers and operators of
vending machines)

Gourmet Tea

Sales of traditional black teas are stagnating in the U.S. due to an aging population that is losing interest in caffeine and increasing competition from newly popular gourmet coffee. Gourmet upscale teas, however, may began to grow in popularity just as gourmet coffee has. Dat-

THE CONSUMER

ing back thousands of years, tea cultivation has a significant established cultural record from which to nourish this growth.

The Chinese and Asian teas currently available in the U.S. represent a small fraction of the thousands of varieties available. Teas with the most well-established reputation for taste quality include those from the Uva district of Ceylon; Assam varieties from Numalighur, Paneery, and other gardens (tea plantations) in India; first flush Darjeeling teas from the Glenburn, Namring, or other estates in India; Fancy Oolong from Taiwan; Ti Kuan Yin Oolong tea from China; Gu Zhang Mao Jian green tea from China; and Gyokuro-grade green tea from Japan.

Mass-market tea trends, on the other hand, have less to do with gourmet tastes than with convenience. The fastest-growing mass-market segment is prepared iced tea. Sales of these products, which are packaged in bottles, cans, and cartons, increased 50 percent in 1992. Prepared teas are a relatively new product type in the United States, although they have been established in Japan for many years.

According to the Tea Council of the United States, sales of prepared teas now account for about 7 percent of the total tea market. The balance of sales are from teas for brewing and powdered, instant varieties. A report from Marketing Intelligence Service Ltd. indicates about 200 new prepared teas debuted in 1991 and 1992. Those introductions, coupled with heavy advertising, are likely to mean continued growth for prepared teas. Because of the potential negative effect of prepared teas on cola sales and the promise of new profits from the teas, the major cola companies are getting in on the act with prepared teas of their own. Pepsi owns Lipton, Coca-Cola owns Nestea, and A&W owns Tetley.

RESOURCES:

Eden Foods, Inc.
Clinton, MI
(517) 456-7424
(imported teas)

The Tea Council of the United States
New York, NY
(212) 986-6998
(industry association of tea boards from tea-producing countries promoting tea consumption in the U.S.)

The Republic of Tea
Mill Valley, CA
(415) 721-2177
(imported teas)

The Republic of Tea Book of Tea and Herbs
by The Republic of Tea
Cole Group Editions, 1993
(707) 538-0492
$12, 160 pages

Vintage Beer

Special brews of beer that are aged for years before drinking may soon attract more attention from taste-conscious beer lovers. The brews, known as vintage beers, are produced in a limited number of breweries around the world, including ones in Great Britain, Belgium, and Switzerland. The aged brews are usually stored for at least a year before serving. Vintages can range from 6 months to 25 years.

These special beers are bottled without being filtered as most mass-market brews are and undergo additional fermentation while being stored. The aging process intensifies the flavor, color, and alcoholic content. Thomas Hardy Ale, a vintage beer brewed in England, has had past mention in the *Guiness Book of World Records* as the world's strongest beer—it has more than 10 percent alcohol. This and other aged beers in Great Britain are traditionally referred to as barley wines.

Vintage beer is unlikely to have a significant impact on the beer industry in the U.S. because it is made in such limited quantities. If makers of the brews do try to make inroads in this country, they could face an uphill marketing battle. Their aged beers will compete against the product of the nation's microbreweries, which tout the freshness of their brews. This aged-versus-freshness perception could confuse some customers.

Thanks to their growing popularity, microbrewed and specialty beers now generate about $500 million annually. That still is only a fraction of the $14 billion spent on beer in this country each year. Microbrews have been so successful that some of their makers now exceed the microbrewery production standard of 20,000 barrels or less a year. These include Anchor Steam, Sierra Nevada, Samuel Adams, and New Amsterdam.

One trend coming out of the microbrewery industry is the use of larger bottles for beer. "Bombers," 22-ounce bottles, have long been popular with home brewers, and now some major brewers are considering this size container.

Even as microbrewed beers grow in popularity and sales, the mass-produced varieties are seeing their sales decline. This is largely due to the aging population and a cyclical decrease in the number of prime beer drinkers—18-to-26-year-olds. To increase profits, major breweries like Miller, Heileman, Rolling Rock, and Coors are introducing specialty brews of their own. Some mass-brewers may even acquire established microbreweries to establish more credibility and profits in this market segment.

RESOURCES:

Association of Brewers
Boulder, CO
(303) 447-0816
(industry association of individuals, manufacturers, retailers, and wholesalers of specialty beers)

Other Beverage Trends

FRUIT PUNCH Fruit flavoring continues to gain appeal among consumers. Beverage makers will add new fruit varieties in 1994, including extensions of existing cola and noncarbonated drink lines. Most of the recent growth in fruit-flavored drinks has come from the "New Age" beverages—clear, carbonated waters with a minimum of fruit flavoring. Although this category has been growing at about 10 percent a year—compared with annual growth for traditional colas of less than 2 percent a year—it has increasing competition from clear colas, spring and mineral waters, bottled teas, and other drinks. New Age drinks generate an estimated $700 million in sales annually. The newest flavors to be mass-marketed are cranberry and lemon.

CUSTOM WATER The quenching of upscale thirsts with expensive bottled waters is a trend that has gone through several phases in the last few decades. Most recently, major brands such as Perrier have been supplanted by smaller, more exclusive brands that often come and go quickly. Many gourmet restaurants have cashed in on this trend by stocking a selection of specialty bottled waters, and in the most recent trend, some have even created their own private brands.

NEW KICK FOR CAFFEINE Instant and decaffeinated coffees have lost some steam with consumers over the past year. The primary reasons are real or perceived deficiencies in taste and the rapid growth of fresh-ground-coffee outlets. These retail stores are giving coffee sales a boost. This trend, originating in the Northwest, is spreading through the Midwest and East. The effect on supermarket sales of packaged coffees so far has been negligible, except for the noted drop-off in sales for decaffeinated brews. But supermarkets are also cashing in on the trend. Many large stores and chains have added or will soon add a greater selection of fresh-roasted coffee beans and flavored varieties. Sales of fresh-roasted beans to grocery stores by Brothers Gourmet Products alone are increasing 25 percent a year. Coming soon: more consumer demand for green coffee beans for roasting at home.

RESOURCES:

National Coffee Association
of the U.S.A.
New York, NY
(212) 344-5596
(industry association of coffee importers, distributors, packagers, and processors)

Brothers Gourmet Products
Denver, CO
(303) 375-0828
(coffee packager)

Beverage Industry
published by Stagnito Publishing Company
North Brook, IL
(708) 205-5660

Beverage World
published by Keller International Publishing Corporation
Great Neck, NY
(516) 829-9210

THE CONSUMER

Cooking and Cleaning

Sales of microwave ovens have slowed considerably, largely due to market saturation. As the echo baby boom grows up, however, they will establish enough new households to boost microwave sales. There should also be demand for units to replace aging, inefficient models and for multiple units for homes and offices.

Most changes in microwave ovens in the coming year will be in style, not technology. New looks are white on white or black on black and color coordination between appliances and cabinets. The only technological innovation in the works is from Whirlpool, which has developed an oven that uses multiple wave patterns to heat more evenly.

One of the failings of microwaves—their inability to turn out high-quality baked goods—may be remedied soon. An improved leavening agent for microwavable baked goods has been developed by Rhone-Poulenc, Inc. This leavening relies on reformulated standard baking powders with the addition of new ingredients that make it well-suited to the shortened baking times of microwave products.

Microwaves may soon be expanding from cooking food to disposing of it, thanks to the microwave garbage disposal. Currently available only in Japan from Matsushita Electrical Industrial Company, this device uses microwave heating to reduce organic debris to ashes. Problems with these devices include the high purchase price of $3,800 and excessive use of electricity. Microwave disposals are not expected to be available in the U.S. in the near future.

Beyond the kitchen, commercial availability of microwave clothes dryers is nearing. Their energy efficiency may spark a major replacement trend. Preliminary tests of a prototype unit from Micro-Tech, Inc. have shown the dryer is safe, performs well on a variety of fabrics, works at lower temperatures than conventional dryers, and dries clothes in less time. Another microwave dryer is being developed by the Electric Power Research Institute. The new dryers may be available within another year, and prices should be slightly higher than for conventional units. Prices will come down, though, as more of these dryers are manufactured.

RESOURCES:

Whirlpool Corporation
Benton Harbor, MI
(616) 926-5000
(home-appliance manufacturer)

Rhone-Poulenc Rorer
Food Ingredients Division
Collegeville, PA
(215) 454-8000
(microwave leavening agent)

Electric Power Research Institute
Palo Alto, CA
(415) 855-2000
(industry association of electric utility companies)

NEW CONVENTIONS IN STOVES Some changes are on the way for conventional ranges and ovens. Sealed gas burners of stainless-steel construction should be available on more mid-priced units. Mixed-fuel stoves that have gas burners and electric ovens are on the way, as well as electronic stove controls and more affordable induction-top stoves priced at less than $1,000.

RESOURCES:

Association of Home Appliance
Manufacturers
Chicago, IL
(312) 984-5800
(industry association of appliance manufacturers and suppliers)

FILLING UP ON REFILLS Consumer interest in recycling may be widespread, but actions indicate the interest may be a mile wide and an inch deep. Despite fervent support for the concept of a healthier environment, relatively little effort is being spent implementing recycling nationwide.

One exception is a trend in the packaging industry. Consumers have embraced products sold with less packaging and those packaged with more "ecologically friendly" materials. Many packagers have switched to refillable containers and flexible pouches for some consumer products, especially household cleaners.

Even though consumers want to purchase products in environmentally friendly packaging, they may resist if certain practical considerations are not addressed by these new packages. These include flexible containers that stand up, pouring spouts for refilling, and strength and durability.

RESOURCES:

Packaging
published by Cahners Publishing
Company
Des Plaines, IL
(708) 635-8800
(packaging-industry trade
publication)

Long Live the Auto

Since the beginning of the automotive industry, car ownership has entailed the almost-constant repair and replacement of auto components. Items such as tires, brakes, shock absorbers, spark plugs, and mufflers have required constant monitoring and replacement, no matter how expensive or exclusive the model.

Earlier in the auto era, three years marked the point after which increasing repairs made it more practical to buy a new vehicle than fix an older one, according to some industry analysts. Today, however, improvements in manufacturing techniques, materials, and rustproofing have made the practical life of a car about five years, and the reliability of three-year-old vehicles is estimated to be increasing at about 5 percent a year, according to a Boston Consulting Group research report.

As the reliability of cars increases, so too does their value in the used-car market. Since 1989, sales of used cars have outpaced sales of new cars, a change driven by increasing consumer trust in vehicles with miles on their odometers. Program cars—low-mileage vehicles used for a few months by rental companies and sold back to dealers—are also enticing used-car shoppers. Program cars are sold with limited manufacturer's warranties and can be substantially less expensive than a new car of the same model.

Many new-car dealers, however, are taking a beating due to the improved reliability of cars and sales of program cars. Dealerships number about 23,000 now, half as many as 50 years ago. Manufacturers are likely to try to stop this slide by extending the use period before program vehicles can be resold to dealers and by limiting the number of cars included in large sales packages to car-rental companies. Nonetheless, additional car makers, like Nissan, Toyota, and Honda, have started selling program cars and should have more units available in 1994.

The increasing number of consumers who lease new cars is also putting downward pressure on new-car sales. In the five-year period between 1988 and 1992, leasing has increased from 17 percent to 22 percent of new-car sales. At least one estimate in the industry projects the leasing rate to hit 30 percent by 1997 (CNW Marketing Research). Leasing is gaining popularity primarily because consumers can no longer deduct interest on installment loans such as car loans.

The Ford Motor Company aggressively markets its leasing program, especially for Taurus models. In 1992, Taurus leases accounted for about 30 percent of all vehicle deliveries, making this model a bellwether for leasing in the industry. Ford is expected to accelerate the marketing of its leasing program even more in 1994, possibly airing an infomercial on the advantages of leasing. (See also "Infomercials," page 160.)

Luxury-car sales have suffered from the lackluster national economy, as well as from the growing popularity and status of sport-utility vehicles. So manufacturers like BMW, Porsche, Mercedes, and Jaguar are touting the budgetary advantages of leasing to their upscale consumers. An increased number of leased luxury vehicles may backfire on luxury makers, though. With the typical two-year leasing period, the large numbers of cars returned to sales floors at the end of leasing periods could drive down the average price, encouraging consumers to buy these bargain vehicles instead of the latest models.

RESOURCES:

Boston Consulting Group, Inc.
Boston, MA
(617) 973-1200
(management consulting services)

CNW Marketing Research, Inc.
Bandon, OR
(503) 347-4718
(marketing research)

National Automobile Dealers
Association
McLean, VA
(703) 821-7000
(industry association of franchised new-car and truck dealers)

Automotive Information Council
Herndon, VA
(703) 713-0700
(industry association of suppliers and manufacturers of cars and car parts)

Automotive Fleet and Leasing
Association
Ford Motor Company
Redondo Beach, CA
(310) 376-8788
(industry association of car-leasing companies and consultants)

Other Automobile Trends

NEW MODELS Auto makers are cranking out improved cars in 1994. These include the Neon from Chrysler, an economy car for both Dodge and Plymouth that includes dual-front air bags, a performance engine, and improved side-impact collision protection. At General Motors, Chevrolet will be resurrecting the Impala name in 1994, using it on a special edition of the Caprice. The new model will feature a Corvette power plant, bucket seats, and a handling system borrowed from the police version of the Caprice. The 1995 model of the Lumina Coupe will be renamed the Monte Carlo. Ford is planning a major redesign of the Taurus and Sable, which may include a longer wheelbase and shorter overall body length. And the 1995 BMW roadster will be made at the company's new plant in Spartanburg, South Carolina.

TWO-STROKE ENGINES Improvements have been reported in the development of a commercially acceptable two-stroke engine for passenger cars. Companies working on this technology include General Motors, Chrysler, Jaguar, Toyota, and Honda. Two-stroke engines are desirable because they are smaller, lighter, and burn less fuel to produce the same amount of power as the four-stroke engines currently used in most cars. Though the emissions problems previously characteristic of the two-stroke engine have been eliminated, the engines are noisier than four-stroke engines and are motor-oil guzzlers. The engines may be in place in passenger cars in two to three years as these problems are overcome with technological improvements.

ELECTRICAL UPDATE Progress is being reported in the development of a viable commercial electric car. Pressure from the impending California state deadline for reduced fleet-vehicle emissions is helping to move this technology closer to the public market. The first commercial vehicles will likely appear in 1994 but in limited numbers and regions. Widespread availability of "volts-wagons" could happen by 1996.

RECYCLABLE INSTRUMENT PANEL Dow Chemical Company has developed a new instrument panel from lightweight, recyclable plastics. The panel is inexpensive to manufacture and easy to recycle, and protects passengers in accidents.

THE CONSUMER

FUEL STANDARDS The U.S. Department of Transportation's new fuel-economy standards, referred to as Corporate Average Fuel Economy standards, or CAFE, will go into effect for 1995 car and light-truck models. However, lobbying and political pressure have delayed the final decision about what the standard will be. Current estimates are 21.0 miles per gallon for automobiles and 20.6 mpg for light trucks. Unless the price of gasoline increases dramatically—not forecast to happen at this point—consumers will most likely take little notice of this change. Performance will still be more attractive than fuel consumption.

GADGET TECHNOLOGY New-car technologies that should appear in the next two model years include a rearview mirror that measures glare from headlights and automatically dims the mirror in response and neon-powered turn signals that improve visibility.

RESOURCES:

Dow Automotive Materials Division
Southfield, MI
(313) 358-1300
(plastic materials for automobiles)

Department of Transportation
Washington, DC
(202) 366-4000
(government department
monitoring CAFE standards)

Donnelly Corporation
Holland, MI
(616) 786-7000
(glass-related automotive products)

Osram Sylvania, Inc.
Hillsboro, NH
(800) 258-3776
(lighting products)

The Retail Environment

The pace of expansion in the shopping-mall industry may never again approach the boom years of the past few decades. In fact, few really large enclosed malls are likely to be built in the U.S. during the remainder of the decade because of oversaturation and a glut of shopping opportunities throughout most of the country. At the same time, recent economic conditions have also had a negative effect on sales, which have dropped by more than 7 percent over the last three years at the largest malls.

Although the recent opening of the largest mall in the U.S., the Mall of America in Bloomington, Minnesota, has so far proven a success, this exception may help prove the rule. Other malls in the area have already noted a drop-off in their revenue, the result of their neighbor's greater draw.

The Mall of America offers more than shopping; it offers entertainment. Entertainment, in fact, has been one of the bulwarks of shopping-center appeal since the first flush of shopping enthusiasm subsided. The latest trend in entertainment draws for malls is activity-based centers, especially interactive games, redemption games (see also "Arcades," page 163), family-oriented sports such as miniature golf, kiddie rides, roller skating, pool and billiards, and some sports-oriented activities such as batting cages, golf simulators, climbing walls, and even nontraditional "sports" such as Velcro jumping.

Trends in shopping centers for 1994 will include increased use of part-time help, higher occupancy costs, longer business hours, more special-event sales, more frequent-buyer programs, and increasing retailer reliance on power centers and neighborhood centers over regional malls.

RESOURCES:

International Council of Shopping
Centers
New York, NY
(212) 421-8181
(industry association of shopping-
center developers, owners,
managers, and retailers)

International Mass Retail
Association
Washington, DC
(202) 861-0774
(industry association of discount
retail chains)

Other Mall Trends

REPLICA MALLS Instead of traveling to distant locations to shop, some new mall designs are bringing the look and feel of special locations to the local shopping center. One such facility in Los Angeles, CityWalk, opened in 1993. It features a shopping promenade modeled after the city's own noted features, including Venice Beach, Olvera Street, and Sunset Boulevard. This also blurs the distinction between shopping and entertainment by providing a theme-oriented style to the shopping environment, adding features such as museums and new amusement-park-style ride simulators.

MALL EXPORTS Mall developers may be in a slump in the U.S., but business south of the border is brisk. Mexico is in the midst of an economic expansion, at least at the middle-class consumer level. The anticipated arrival of the North American Free Trade Agreement (NAFTA) will make business and travel to Mexico easier for retailers and consumers (see "Mexican Vacations," page 234). According to those who are developing retail activity in Mexico, however, NAFTA is not the deciding factor. Delays in passage of the legislation will not have a substantial effect on moves already underway. Retail expansion into Mexico currently includes Arby's, Chili's, Dillard's, Domino's Pizza, Dryclean USA, The Gap, J.C. Penney, Kmart, Pizza Inn, Price Company, Sam's Club, and Sears. Large projects include three malls in Mexico City—each more than 1 million square feet—being developed by Melvin Simon & Associates.

ETHNOCENTRIC SHOPPING For major ethnic groups in the U.S., population and economic growth have created a position of consumer strength, attracting the attention of retail developers. In various parts of the country, targeted ethnic shopping centers are being created to appeal to specific population groups, most notably African Americans, Asian Americans, and Hispanic Americans.

In practice, this involves recognizing where the "melting pot" ends and cultural identity begins. Because of rising income levels among middle-class ethnic groups, such awareness may also parallel marketing decisions for similar white majority shopping areas. In a few extreme cases, ethnocentric shopping centers cater to the requirements of immigrant groups such as Japanese, Koreans, and Vietnamese, including dietary preferences, music, and foreign-language films. In general, however, efforts target native-born Americans with ethnic roots.

RESOURCES:

Stores
published by National Retail
Federation
New York, NY
(212) 244-8780

National Retail Federation, Inc.
New York, NY
(212) 244-8780
(industry association of retail stores)

THE CONSUMER

Franchise Futures

More than 500,000 franchise locations now serve more than 65 industries and involve an estimated 3,000 franchise companies. Franchises are expected to continue to grow through the 1990s; recent average growth in sales has been about 15 percent a year. Most important, franchising has entered a period of stability. Almost 97 percent of franchise locations opened in the past five years are still in business.

Making up for overexpansion and sloppy business practices common in the past two decades, the franchising segment now has more control over its component practices, from capital investment to management training. Recent surveys of franchise owners indicate a high level of satisfaction with their business arrangements. These indicators suggest a healthy future.

Franchise trends include expanding the concept of franchise business as a segment of business education, developing new systems for product and service flexibility, shrinking staffs and overhead at parent franchise operations, increasing autonomy and decision making for franchise owners, and expanding "retro-franchising"—independent retailers who accept franchised involvement in exchange for capital.

RESOURCES:

National Association of Franchise Companies
Hollywood, FL
(305) 966-1530
(industry association of franchising businesses)

Consultants International Association
Memphis, TN
(901) 761-3085
(industry association of consultants specializing in franchises)

Superstores vs. Convenience

A store concept that has defied the recent slowdown in retail sales is the superstore, a category of specialty retail outlets with 10,000 square feet or more of floor space and a wide variety of products in their specialty category. Superstores were first introduced in the mid-1980s, but have only recently begun to peak in their impact on the retail industry. Rapid growth, in fact, has already had a negative impact on some superstores in the office-supplies category. Between 1986 and 1992, the number of office-products retail companies declined by 45 percent, the result of mergers and store closings.

Superstores are differentiated from warehouse stores less by prices than by decor; that is, they tend to have a more pleasant, well-designed environment. Superstores are often freestanding, but some use existing malls to expand storefront locations into superstore sizes. World Foot Locker and The Limited are two national chains that have enlarged mall locations into superstores.

One of the latest examples of superstores is from the Tandy Corporation (owners of Radio Shack). Its latest oversized outlet, The Incredible Universe, opened in 1993 in Arlington, Texas. This 165,000-square-foot store has a full line of home electronics, including 342 TV models, 72 VCRs, 400 mobile electronic devices, and 579 household appliances, in addition to computer furniture, video games, and toys. More than 300 salespeople work the floor. Tandy also plans to open superstores in other parts of the country beginning with Wilsonville, Oregon, a suburb of Portland.

Other retailers with superstores open or in the planning stages include Media Play (40,000 square feet of sales space owned by the Musicland Group), Blockbuster Video (30,000 square feet—seven new outlets in 1994-95), Petsmart (offering pet food and supplies), Barnes & Noble (see also "Superstores," page 177), FabriCenters of America (16,000 square feet of fabrics and sewing supplies), and Autosource (20,000 square feet of auto supplies and accessories).

Retail industry analysts expect the superstore concept to continue to grow through the rest of the decade, but not without some side effects. Aside from problems the office-products category has already experienced because of rapid growth and competition, some consumers are moving away from the "bigger is better" phenomenon for practical reasons. Stopping at a superstore to pick up a single item may require much more time parking, walking, and standing in line than many consumers are willing to spend.

The convenience factor has already been observed in some retail areas, with grocery stores, office supplies, and hardware outlets picking up sales at the expense of nearby superstores. One new category exemplifies the anti-superstore trend. Bestsellers is a home-entertainment store concept from Canada; its first U.S. stores opened in 1993. Bestsellers offers only the top 20 to 40 best-selling titles for books, magazines, videos, and music. (See also "Book Trends," page 175.) The Tandy Corporation, too, is not abandoning small-store concepts in favor of the superstore. At the same time it expands The Incredible Universe, it is planning a new system of mini-stores for some of its electronics goods. The new ventures, called "Radio Shack Express," are expected to be about three-quarters the size of existing Radio Shack outlets. The company will also reportedly try a similar approach with its Computer City stores.

Service may be as important as convenience in some consumers' shift of allegiance to smaller stores. Wal-Mart, despite its own promotion as a people-friendly shopping attraction, has begun to feel the effects of a backlash in some regions. Despite the low prices, other local merchants, especially grocers, are picking up some Wal-Mart customers because of their smaller size, more personal service, and sometimes, local politics. Service, too, is affecting superstores such as Barnes & Noble in the book industry, where the mandate for low overhead reduces customer service to a minimum, elevating the effectiveness of smaller, independent bookstores or competing independent superstores with more personnel.

Furthermore, some products are not completely represented in superstore formats. Fashion-forward tastes, for instance, may get second billing in clothing superstores in favor of mass production and cloned lines. For fashion-conscious shoppers, small boutiques may always have an edge.

RESOURCES:

National Association of Recording Merchandisers
Marlton, NJ
(609) 596-2221
(industry association of retailers selling recorded entertainment products)

National Office Products Association
Alexandria, VA
(703) 549-9040
(industry association of suppliers, manufacturers, retailers, and wholesalers of office supplies and furniture)

Blockbuster Entertainment Corporation
Fort Lauderdale, FL
(305) 524-8200
(video-tape-rental chain)

Bestsellers
Toronto, Ontario
(416) 593-8857
(entertainment products retail chain)

FabriCenters of America, Inc.
Hudson, OH
(216) 656-2600
(houseware products retail chain)

Auto Source, Inc.
Indianapolis, IN
(317) 328-2886
(automotive supplies retail chain)

Barnes & Noble, Inc.
New York, NY
(212) 633-3300
(trade-books retail chain)

Musicland Group, Inc.
Minneapolis, MN
(612) 932-7700
(recorded-music retail chain)

Retail Automation

Technology has already affected the way retailers handle consumers. From electronic credit checks to bar codes, computers and technology have been implemented in the ongoing quest to improve efficiency, productivity, and service. Advances in technology will soon improve retail operations even more.

A trend that parallels general improvements in office-paper handling and storage is paperless systems at the retail level. These involve reducing or eliminating billing forms, invoices, receipts, and other documents. For many franchised and chain stores, this reduction is accomplished with the addition of more efficient direct electronic links between stores, suppliers, warehouses, and company offices. Links range from high-speed telephone data lines to sophisticated fiber-optic and direct-satellite connections. New software programs reduce the time required to implement paperless retailing. (See also "Electronic Archives," page 93.)

For the retail industry to move toward a paperless business, it will need to adopt standards. Several prototype standards have been studied for use in motor-carrier data interchange, a vital part of the retailing environment. Motor-carrier data interchange is the category of information transmission that involves retailers, wholesalers, shipping companies, and the vehicles used to move merchandise. A few large retail operations already use proprietary shipping standards, but these are not part of the larger model for paperless retailing. The volume of transactions required of the largest retailers in shipping freight suggests there are great benefits to using electronic data interchange. J.C. Penney already transmits more than 100,000 electronic invoices in a typical month. Industry-wide adoption of one or more standards is expected within a few years.

Within stores, electronic improvements include adapting wireless technology to link individual point-of-sale registers and central computers. One advantage to wireless terminals is that you can add or move registers at any time without rerouting data cables. Store chains testing or planning wireless upgrades include J.C. Penney and Mervyns.

With or without wireless connections, more stores will use networking environments. Currently, most networks are merely in-store loops that allow a central computer or workstation to monitor and upload

THE CONSUMER

sales data from individual registers. In expanded usage, networks will link customer data files to individual terminals and connect sales personnel through e-mail and other communications formats.

Another form of wireless catching on quickly is portable wireless point-of-sale (POS). Wireless POS devices combine bar-code scanners, mini-registers, magnetic stripe scanners for credit cards, and receipt printers. Sales clerks can scan items, total sales including taxes, and print receipts for customers while they are standing in line or at a sales display. Mervyns began testing portable POS in 1992—the first retailer in the U.S. to do so—using a system developed by Symbol Technologies; these prototypes are used only for credit-card sales.

In the generation of retail networks just becoming available, individual registers link with suppliers, warehouses, and customer databases, increasing the potential for sales and service. Such "live" hookups also permit more detailed, real-time analysis of sales patterns, customer demographics, and other useful data. System-wide networks are expected to improve merchandise reordering efficiency, automating decisions that might otherwise take days or weeks.

RESOURCES:

Federation of Automated Coding
Technologies
Pittsburgh, PA
(412) 963-8588
(industry association of suppliers
and manufacturers of equipment
and systems used for automatic
identification of products)

Symbol Technologies, Inc.
Bohemia, NY
(516) 563-2400
(code-based data capture systems)

Bar-Code Boosters

Bar codes, the ubiquitous striped tags now on most products sold in the U.S., celebrated their 28th anniversary in 1993. Officially managed as the Universal Product Code (UPC), bar-code use will continue to expand as technology enhances its capabilities and efficiency.

Among the changes underway for UPC: smaller, lighter versions of wireless hand-held scanners, allowing quicker inventorying and product identification; hand-held portable POS devices with bar-code scanners (see above); adapters that allow existing registers to use wireless scanning devices; and pen-based computer connections to wireless retail systems.

The predominant format for existing bar codes is a series of parallel stripes that represent product information. The latest version, however, adds a second dimension, so-called "two-dimensional" bar codes (2D), that require a second pass by a laser in a different direction from the first reading pass. The advantage of 2D is that such codes can store much more information than one-dimensional bar codes.

The 2D code is also referred to as a portable data file (PDF) because of its information-carrying capability of up to 1,000 words in a space about the size of a traditional bar code. 2D codes are expected to provide information for shippers, such as contents of packages and shipment manifests. The first device capable of reading 2D code is a laser scanner from Symbol Technologies.

THE CONSUMER

RESOURCES:

Symbol Technologies, Inc.
Bohemia, NY
(516) 563-2400
(code-based data capture systems)

Telxon Corporation
Akron, OH
(216) 867-3700
(portable computer systems)

Other Retail Trends

STOREFRONT KARAOKE Karaoke, the Japanese version of singing along to popular tunes in public, has developed a small but dedicated audience in some American bars and restaurants. Constrained by cultural barriers from becoming as popular here as it is in Japan, karaoke may nevertheless have another marketing trick up its sleeve. The Star Factory provides mall visitors with the opportunity to record their musical efforts. A high-tech resurrection of the wax-disc recording booths of the 1940s, the Star Factory format includes sound-proof rooms and 1,500 background music selections.

SONY RETAIL Sony is developing a new chain of retail outlets for its electronic products. The first store opened in late 1993 in New York

City. The stores will be called Sony Signatures and carry some of the company's existing products, as well as video games and new products allied with the company's movie and television deals.

TGIF SHOPPING A new twist for retailing is "weekend only" shopping. M&J Liquidators has a store in Stamford, Connecticut, that is only open Friday through Sunday. Offering discounted men's clothing in a warehouse format, this retail concept is based on lower overhead and is open only during peak shopping periods.

NORDIC SHOPPING NordicTrack, a successful personal exercise equipment company formerly limited to sales through television ads and direct mail, is experimenting with a retail outlet called ExerScience. This store will offer traditional exercise gear and clothes as well as the latest fitness machines. Other NordicTrack retail ventures will include Healthy Express, offering juices, baked goods, and salads, as well as kitchenware, juicers, and other food appliances. Healthy Express itself is a spin-off concept of Healthy Kitchen, a NordicTrack store that features a full kitchen where staff members prepare healthy foods and demonstrate appliances as part of a sales pitch for cookbooks, kitchen gadgets, and specialty foods.

RETAIL OVERVIEW For 1994, consumers can expect fewer sales; more full-time discounting by major manufacturers; earlier introduction of full-price seasonal merchandise, especially clothing; and relatively small price increases in most categories.

RESOURCES:

Pioneer Laser Entertainment, Inc.
San Pedro, CA
(310) 952-2111
(recorded-music equipment)

NordicTrack, Inc.
Chaska, MN
(612) 448-6987
(home-exercise equipment)

M&J Liquidators
Stamford, CT
(203) 353-3314
(retail clothing)

Sony
Metuchen, NJ
(201) 930-1000
(retail consumer-electronics products)

Melvin Simon & Associates
Indianapolis, IN
(317) 636-1600
(shopping-mall development and management)

Lawn and Garden Trends

The lawn-and-garden industry will continue to benefit from the green-thumb interests of an aging population. An entrenched corps of committed gardeners among Americans aged 50 and older have long been a significant force in this industry, spending more every year on plants and supplies than other groups of gardeners, although they account for only about 3 percent of all gardeners. As baby boomers reach this age, they will boost the gardening industry for years to come. Lawn-and-garden sales have been growing at an annual rate of at least 6 percent; yearly sales are now an estimated $22 billion.

Current trends in gardening range from composting to organic gardening. Even so, organic practices and supplies have failed to catch on in mainstream consumer markets, except in areas where local regulations control disposal of yard waste. Because such laws are expected to proliferate, increasing interest in organic lawn-and-garden products should follow, although analysts in this industry have observed that consumer interest does not always translate into increased sales.

Despite the increasing popularity of gardening, many baby boomers do not have much extra time to devote to this activity. The result is "quick thumb" gardening, an increase in products and practices customized for part-time, erratic home schedules. This includes more sales of bedding plants instead of seeds—Burpee began offering mail-order delivery of bedding plants in 1993—and choosing flowers and vegetables that require less care. More extensive use of timed watering devices also aids time-short gardeners.

A related trend is for many to transform existing lawns and flower gardens into miniature nature preserves. Ecologically driven consumers as well as those just interested in the aesthetics of the wild—are replacing domesticated grasses and flowers with a range of wild varieties. Of greatest interest: local species, from wildflowers to cacti. Special garden designs attract butterflies and other insects, birds, and in some suburban areas, mammals.

SALTY GRASS Lawns near the shore and in other places where groundwater is salty may soon benefit from progress in turf science that has propagated a number of grass types to withstand salt-heavy conditions. "Salt sods" are already used commercially along some roadways where salting is common in winter months. These sods are combinations of grasses such as Dawson red fescue, Galway fescue, Scaldis hard fescue, and Rugby Kentucky bluegrass, all salt-tolerant grasses. The newest and most salt-tolerant is known as the "Fults" cultivar, a type of perennial bunchgrass found growing naturally on a golf course in Colorado.

POTTING CURES Improved mixtures of soils and additives naturally suppress plant diseases sometimes found in potting mixtures. The new disease-suppressive potting soils use mixtures of naturally occurring microorganisms and compounds such as pine bark and lime. Only recently distributed to greenhouses and commercial plant suppliers, the safer soils should be available to consumers within one to two years.

WET THUMBS Pond gardening has been increasing in popularity for the past decade, a natural extension for a maturing population with larger gardens and budgets. One outgrowth of this trend: new interest in water-lily propagation. Traditionally, efforts to create new types of water lilies yielded one or two new hybrids per year; in 1992, 70 appeared.

ORNAMENTAL MUSHROOMS Interest in wild and cultivated mushrooms has been growing rapidly over the past few decades, part of the trend toward natural foods, heartland cooking, and overall gourmet cooking. The latest trend promotes the use of some mushrooms as decorations, along with other wild flora and traditional cultivated flowers. Species originate in Belgium and include Coriolis versicolor, Pholiota spectabilis, and Pholiota brumalis. The usual cautions about not eating certain mushrooms are still in effect.

ORNAMENTAL HOPS The USDA, perhaps anticipating an eventual decline in beer production in this country, has developed a new form of hops plant for ornamental use in gardens. Humulus lupulus, the "Blue Northern Brewer," is an attractive multi-colored vine suitable for growing in most regions, except parts of the deep South. The new ornamental was first made available to nurseries in spring 1993; commercial availability should come within one to two years.

GENERAL GROWTH IN GARDENING Other gardening trends include more gardening products for children, more discount and warehouse-type retailing of garden products, favoring of perennials over annuals, and more custom gardening services. For gardeners seriously committed to this activity, more guides and tours will be offered to check out the competition while on vacation.

RESOURCES:

Garden Club of America
New York, NY
(212) 753-8287
(national organization of amateur gardeners)

The National Gardening Association
Burlington, VT
(802) 863-1308
(industry association of amateur gardening groups)

The Lawn Institute
Marietta, GA
(404) 977-5492
(industry association of business and research organizations working with grass and sod)

Garden Centers of America
Washington, DC
(202) 789-2900
(industry association of owners and operators of retail garden outlets)

International Water Lily Society
Buckeystown, MD
(301) 874-5503
(industry association of amateurs, professionals, and botanical groups involved with water gardening)

Agricultural Research Service
U.S.D.A.
Corvalis, OR
(503) 737-5841
(world hops cultivar collection)

THE CONSUMER

FIVE

ENTERTAINMENT AND THE MEDIA

ENTERTAINMENT AND THE MEDIA

Baby boomers who are having children of their own now are bringing to the fore a new generation of family-oriented movies and, conversely, a decline in the number of violent films. Interactive television is on the way, but America's couch potatoes may not embrace it as the industry hopes.

Television

Based on media coverage in 1992 and 1993, the television industry has seen the future. It is 500-channel interactive systems, and it is coming soon. This description of the future of television has become so widespread that it is considered more fact than observation. Countering this, however, are several important factors that will delay, alter, or possibly kill aspects of this new formula for America's most popular entertainment medium.

500 CHANNELS? Most communities in this country can expect to have expanded choices for programming within the next three to five years. Many communities may then have the capacity to receive as many as 500 channels. Tele-Communications Inc. will be installing the first such system any day, but it will be years, if ever, before all 500 channels have programming other than studio-generated blank screens. At the most, perhaps 100 channels may be offered to some viewers, for a premium price. Most of those channels will offer "multiplexed" staggered viewing schedules for the same movies.

Other systems will duplicate programming with multiple transmissions of the same channels. Community- and service-oriented programming may also fill a few new channels with information such as channel guides, weather reports, community-events listings, and the like.

With the eventual arrival of pay-per-use, a viewer-controlled option to pay only for the programming used, channels could expand. Right now, there are more program channels than the average metropolitan cable system can afford. Pay-per-use would allow access to anything that has been created—Courtroom TV, the Sci-Fi Channel, the Golf Channel, etc., without having to make difficult choices at the system level.

Before then, other uses for unfilled channels may become more attractive. Information services such as telephone directories, library guides, and encyclopedias, now available through online computer connections, could be routed through TV systems. Additional shopping venues could also be added, with sponsoring companies carrying the costs of the programming.

INTERACTIVITY? These services, however, demand unique interactive capabilities so viewers can manipulate the TV image, make choices, answer questions on screen, and otherwise actively engage the program. This type of interaction has great practical applications for both information and entertainment, a fact that has been proven by the success of video games and personal-computer programs. On the other hand, much of the television audience, despite what the industry may think, is not stuck with current old-fashioned programming out of necessity, but because they have chosen it, albeit in a passive way.

The concept of "couch potato" perfectly matches the fulfillment that this distinctive medium provides to most of its viewers. It is exactly the lack of interactivity that makes the format so pleasurable and, in a sense, addictive. Opportunities to "open up" this format to allow couch potatoes to control their viewing environment have so far only made them more efficient at what the medium best provides, passive entertainment. Using remote-control devices, viewers can now graze instead of dine. The end result is the same.

Interactive opportunities for television will be offered in the next few years, despite any practical considerations of their real value. Of the number and variety of efforts underway to milk this technological trend, most are likely to be rather simple information controls, providing viewers with more options to move through their expanded channel capacities, find out what is happening on other channels, and respond to requests for coupons, contests, and surveys.

At least one interactive system will offer controls that mimic those of a VCR, allowing fast-forward, replay, and pause options while watching cable movies. Viacom Inc. will debut its version in 1994 in Castro Valley, California. The simplest, and perhaps most necessary, of interactive functions, a programmable viewing guide, is also close to reality. In 1994, Tele-Communications Inc. will begin testing an interactive video version of *TV Guide* magazine. Accessed through a special remote-control device, it will provide information about program times, categories, contents, and cast members upon request, as well as allowing viewers to preview programs and programming choices.

MICROCASTING With or without interactivity, expanded channel capacity could provide a bonanza for many kinds of marketing services.

With 500 channels available, many at very low cost, advertisers will be able to develop increasingly smaller focus audiences and still make a profit. Such "microcasting," in fact, may put some direct mailers out of business before the end of the decade. At the same time, broadcast television programming will continue to dominate the field in the largest markets, appealing to the broadest segment of the population.

One realm of microcasting that has been building a base of viewers is ethnic programming. A variety of specialized foreign-language channels target those who speak Spanish, Korean, Chinese, Japanese, Arabic, and Hindu. Some programming is already available, but it is usually based on retransmission of existing programs with additional foreign-language soundtracks.

Even as cable systems add channels, they face a major threat from a new generation of satellite broadcast systems. U.S. Satellite Broadcasting Inc. will begin direct broadcast of 60 channels through satellite delivery in 1994. Using a new generation of receiving dishes that are only a few feet square—about the size of a pizza pan—households will be able to receive cable-quality programming from all major cable channels, including MTV, CNN, Nickelodeon, Showtime, HBO, and the Disney Channel. Inital charges for the mini-dishes should be about $700. Prices will drop to less than half that within a few years. Monthly charges will be competitive with most cable fees. The advantage over cable is that viewers have control over which programs they receive. With cable systems, operators make choices from what is available on the system.

RESOURCES:

U.S. Satellite Broadcasting, Inc.
St. Paul, MN
(612) 645-4500
(satellite-delivered programming)

Hughes Communications, Inc.
El Segundo, CA
(310) 607-4511
(satellite-communications services)

Viacom, Inc.
New York, NY
(212) 258-6000
(cable-TV programming)

Tele-Communications, Inc.
Englewood, CO
(303) 267-5500
(cable-television services)

National Cable Television
Association
Washington, DC
(202) 775-3550
(industry association of cable-TV system operators, programmers, and networks)

ENTERTAINMENT
AND THE MEDIA

CABLE CLUTTER As of 1993, U.S. cable and satellite broadcast systems offered an estimated 100 different television channels. Although the average cable system has 60 or fewer channels, some filled with local and broadcast programming, hopeful programmers are continually developing new concepts in the hope that they may win out over existing channels.

Increasing channel capacity will not automatically result in more programs. Most U.S. cable systems may not be able to afford to upgrade to new technology for years, even past the turn of the century. Even then, adding networks to fill channel space will likely be a piecemeal process, a few at a time. The most obvious choices to fill new channel space will be programming that pays for itself, i.e., more pay-per-view options and premium channels.

RESOURCES:

National Cable Television
Association
Washington, DC
(202) 775-3550
(industry association of cable-TV
system operators, programmers,
and networks)

ENTERTAINMENT AND THE MEDIA

New TV Channels

The following are television-programming options that are currently being developed or proposed:

FOX EXPANSION A cooperative venture between Fox Inc. and Tele-Communications Inc. has established a new venue for this broadcast system: TCI cable systems will carry a new Fox-originated channel comprising original and repeat programming.

PBS CHANNEL The Public Broadcasting Service will venture into cable turf in 1994 or 1995 with the introduction of Horizons TV. This cable channel will have cultural and educational programming created by museums, universities, and libraries, consisting of documentaries, lectures, demonstrations, tours, interviews, and some advertising. PBS affiliates WGBH (Boston) and WNET (New York) will provide production and support.

EXERCISE CHANNEL Exercise-oriented viewers may find much to appreciate in FXTV, the Fitness and Exercise Television channel.

SPORTS NEWS CHANNEL A reported spinoff of the popular ESPN sports channel is ESPN II, covering sports news and information.

ECO-TV Two new channels will cover environmental and ecological themes: Planet Central TV Network and the ECO Channel.

HISTORY CHANNEL The Arts & Entertainment Channel will be premiering a new cable venture devoted to historic subjects, H-TV.

ROOTS CHANNEL The World African Network will feature programming about the African continent, including documentaries, interviews, news, politics, nature, and culture.

WAR CHANNEL The Military Channel will focus on armed-forces programming, from war movies to documentaries.

CRIME CHANNEL The Crime Channel will carry programs about criminal activity and crime prevention.

RECOVERY CHANNEL The RecoveryNet channel, a.k.a. "The Wellness Channel," will cover psychological and physiological aspects of recovery from various addictions.

DO-IT-YOURSELF CHANNEL The How-To Channel will cover basic projects for homeowners, from plumbing to painting.

YAK CHANNEL Round-the-clock talking heads will be the main feature on Talk TV.

ROMANCE CHANNEL American Movie Classics expects to launch a new channel on Valentine's Day in 1994. Romance Classics will offer 24-hour programming featuring movies, original productions, and spe-

ENTERTAINMENT
AND THE MEDIA

cial features targeting women aged 25 and older. Also pending: video broadcast versions of popular Harlequin romance novels. Alliance Communications Corporation will adapt the books for TV; the first broadcasts are planned for CBS.

DUFFERS CHANNEL Arnold Palmer is developing the 24-hour Golf Channel, set to debut in 1994.

EATING CHANNEL The brand-new Television Food Network, produced by the Providence Journal Company, features interviews, call-in shows, health, nutrition, and cooking tips.

HOLY ROCK CHANNEL Christian rock and roll is the concept for Z-Music, a channel offering a narrowcast version of MTV.

COMMERCIAL CHANNEL The Advertising Television channel—ATV—expects to offer nonstop commercials.

COMPUTER CHANNEL The Jones Computer Network plans to expand to 24-hour programming. It is now available as a segment of weekly programming on the Mind Extension University (ME/U), a learning channel created by Jones Intercable Company. The new channel will offer guidance for personal computer users, information about computer development, product demonstrations, call-in shows, and on-air lessons that can lead to a degree in computer science (offered by George Washington University). (See also "Distance-Learning Update," page 200.)

BOOKS MEET TV Bestselling author E. L. Doctorow and others in the book industry will be offering Booknet, a 24-hour cable channel devoted to books. The channel will include interviews, reviews, readings, literacy programming, book-industry news, and a Cable Bookstore for on-air sales.

TURNER TWINS Two new channels will debut from Turner Broadcasting. Turner Classic Movies will feature commercial-free films, mostly from the 1930s through the 1950s. CNN International will provide expanded world-news coverage.

MORE PAY CHANNELS More premium cable channels will debut in 1994 from Encore Media Corporation. The new channels will feature movies and special programming in distinctive areas, including action/adventure, mysteries, love stores, Westerns, true stories, and a selection of features aimed at 8-to-16-year-olds. These specialized channels will provide "mood on demand," according to the company, and will cost about $5 per month. The rollout of these new channels is set for mid-1994 through TCI cable systems.

CABLE GAMES The Sega Channel is expected to debut in 1994, providing nonstop video-game programs on TCI cable systems. Time Warner Entertainment is also involved in this deal, which will require special devices that users connect to their cable systems so they can download game software. Initial estimates of added fees for this service are $15-20 per month. Another cable video game venture is the Game Show Channel from United Video and Sony.

ONLINE COMPUTER HYBRID The Prodigy System, an online information and entertainment service used by a reported 1 million personal-computer owners, is planning a cable television version of its programming. The new Prodigy Channel would allow TV viewers to interact with information sources the way they can on personal computers. Programming would include news, games, electronic shopping, bulletin boards, and sports scores.

COMMUNITY PROGRAMMING OPTIONS A proposed programming venture expects to provide public-affairs programs to local cable-TV systems. An estimated 15,000 hours of community programming are produced and shown locally every year. National Community Network, Inc. is raising capital to develop a nationwide distribution system that offers a mix of local programming from around the country, nationally produced public-affairs programs, and general informational programming.

ENTERTAINMENT AND THE MEDIA

RESOURCES:

ESPN, Inc.
Bristol, CT
(203) 585-2242
(sports programming)

Planet Central TV Network
Malibu, CA
(310) 317-4500
(environmental programming)

ECO Channel
Ellicott City, MD
(410) 750-7291
(environmental programming)

H-TV
New York, NY
(212) 661-4500
(history programming)

World African Network
Los Angeles, CA
(213) 299-3300
(African programming)

The Military Channel
Louisville, KY
(502) 425-8161
(military programming)

The Crime Channel
Van Nuys, CA
(818) 907-5769
(crime and mystery programming)

The RecoveryNet Channel
Milwaukee, WI
(414) 771-2288
(psychological programming)

Talk TV
Paradise Valley, AZ
(602) 585-1515
(interview programming)

Romance Classics
Woodbury, NY
(516) 364-2222
(romance programming)

Golf Channel
Birmingham, AL
(205) 995-0910
(golf programming)

Television Food Network
New York, NY
(212) 586-1731
(food programming)

Z-Music
Lake Haven, FL
(904) 228-1000
(Christian music programming)

Jones Computer Network
Englewood, CO
(303) 792-3111
(computer programming)

Booknet
New York, NY
(212) 698-7808
(book programming)

Turner Broadcasting System
Atlanta, GA
(404) 827-1500
(movie and news programming)

Encore Media Corporation
Denver, CO
(303) 771-7700
(specialized programming)

Sega Channel
New York, NY
(212) 484-6767
(video-game programming)

Prodigy Channel
White Plains, NY
(914) 993-8000
(information programming)

National Community Network
Houston, TX
(713) 932-9178
(community programming)

Other Television Trends

SAFE SEX After several decades of rapid growth, cable television is ensconced in the majority of American households and has survived some controversy along the way. Despite objections in many localities over sexually explicit programming—the Playboy Channel has received the brunt of the criticism—much of the furor has died down. So has the Playboy Channel, replaced by successful pay-per-view options. Channels such as Spice, Playboy, and Hot Choice offer "soft-porn" that is reportedly much less revealing than many titles widely available at video-rental stores. This pay-per-view programming offers more control to both local systems and individual households. This "safety" factor should help maintain growth for this segment. Adult services are already generating as much as half of the revenues in some local cable systems.

REALITY TV HITS THE WALL Reality programming—cop shows, news magazines, exposés, amateur video, real-life adventures, etc.—now faces over-saturation. Furthermore, advertisers are increasingly favoring family audiences, and family programming. On the upswing: family shows, low-violence adventures, nature programming.

COSTLY PREMIUMS Premium and pay-per-view channels are likely to face fee hikes in 1994. These channels are exempt from fee increases controlled by the Cable Act of 1992.

MINISERIES MINIBOOM A new crop of miniseries will appear in the next few TV seasons, including one based on the *Rabbitt* novels by John Updike. Others will include Alexandra Ripley's *Scarlett*, a sequel to "Lonesome Dove," a sequel to "North and South," a sequel to "The Thorn Birds," a series based on the life of King Arthur, and an miniseries called "Madonna: The Early Years."

OTHER NEW ARRIVALS Kevin Costner will produce "Five Hundred Nations" a documentary series of native-American history for CBS. "Babylon 5," a new sci-fi series, will debut in January 1994. Time Warner will introduce "Entertainment News Television." "The Price is Right," a popular prime-time game show that aired from 1957 to 1964 before moving to day-time syndication, will be revived in the evening hours in 1994 with new host Doug Davidson.

Shopping through Television

INFOMERCIALS Infomercials have passed a threshold test in the past few years. Despite some complaints about style, content, and business practices, they have endured long enough to establish a permanent niche for themselves in television programming. They can no longer be dismissed as a temporary fad.

More and larger companies are moving into this advertising format, or at least exploring it with more energy. For purveyors of low-cost consumer products, the proof is in the numbers. Infomercial sales in the United States totaled $350 million in 1988. In 1993, estimated sales reached $900 million, a gain of almost 300 percent. In 1994, annual sales are expected to reach or pass $1.2 billion. In comparison, sales of products through television shopping channels were $2 billion in 1992.

In 1992, 150 infomercial productions aired on domestic TV channels. The number is expected to reach 200 by the end of 1994. These numbers, however, may hide a high failure rate. Some industry analysts believe that only one in ten infomercials makes a profit.

One of the most noticeable changes in infomercials as they become more successful is in their length of run. In infomercials' early days, a single "episode" would air for 9 to 12 months. Now, some infomercials are becoming more like regular television programming, with fresh "episodes" appearing on a more regular basis. In 1994, some products and companies are expected to release new versions of programs on a monthly basis.

Another emerging trend to look for in infomercials is different products sharing air time. Such cooperative infomercials may also include segments with coordinated themes—jewelry, exercise, beauty aids, etc.—like those now common on shopping networks.

Other infomercial trends include more spots designed to generate sales leads and marketing contacts instead of sales that ask callers to leave contact information in order to receive brochures or other material; use of infomercials as an extended standard advertisement for national brands; and education of consumers about new products rather than just to produce sales. Walt Disney World and Dayton Hudson stores are already experimenting or planning moves into infomercials to introduce new concepts or promote existing ones.

HOME SHOPPING Only nine years after the first national broadcast of the televised shopping concept, The Home Shopping Club (HSC), based in St. Petersburg, Florida, reports it has 5 million Club members. QVC (standing for Quality, Value, Convenience), the other major shopping channel, began broadcasting in 1986 and logs a reported 100,000 new customers per month—1.2 million per year. Sixty percent of these viewers became regular buyers.

Home-shopping networks will also undergo some changes in 1994, one of which will be invisible to American audiences. In recent years, privatization of state-run television programming has opened the door to entrepreneurial expansion in many European countries. One of the first entries to step through will be various versions of product sales on television. Countries with home-shopping programming already underway or soon to arrive include Estonia, Finland, Germany, Latvia, Lithuania, Italy, Spain, Sweden, and the United Kingdom. One impediment, especially in the formerly Communist bloc countries, is the widespread lack of credit cards, the most practical way to buy things from TV.

The U.S. clearly doesn't have this problem. The general trend in television shopping is an increased ceiling for purchase prices. Initial shopper limits kept most products close to $20, because viewers were not willing to spend more through these services in their early days. Currently, TV shopping channels report success with most products at a ceiling of about $50. Some anticipate that this level will rise in coming years, adding potentially larger items to the TV shopping list.

ONLINE AND BEYOND The TV connection between consumers and products has obviously proven effective and popular. Not so, as least so far, for related connections using personal computers. Online shopping services range from groceries to classified ads and include some of the same products offered on television-shopping programs, but success has so far been elusive. According to one estimate, only about $100 million in product purchases are accounted for through the estimated 4 million computer users who participate in online services, versus the $2 billion spent through TV shopping connections in 1992.

ENTERTAINMENT AND THE MEDIA

MicroMall offers a new interactive shopping service halfway between television and computers. Using technology from Bell Atlantic Directory Services, freestanding video kiosks will be placed in shopping centers, hotel lobbies, transportation terminals, and other public locations. Viewers use an interactive videodisc to scan images of products, search for items, listen to a voice track, and make purchases with credit cards. Purchased items are shipped to the customer's home. Initial use includes products from traditional direct mailers such as Spiegel, J.C. Penney, Lands' End, and Hammacher Schlemmer. The first MicroMall units were installed in mid-1993 in Chicago and Wilmington, Delaware.

OTHER TRENDS IN TV SHOPPING Ventures include TV Macy's, to debut in fall in 1994, featuring products from Macy's stores and programming shot on location at stores around the country. Nordstrom's, the Seattle-based retail chain, is also exploring the possibility of a shopping channel. Others with similar interests include the Spiegel Catalog and the Sharper Image, although these ventures could end up as regularly scheduled programs on existing shopping networks such as QVC. Despite the lure of potential profits, retailers are mindful of the J.C. Penney home-shopping venture, a project that was slow to generate sales and was dropped in mid-1990.

RESOURCES:

Bell Atlantic Directory Services
Philadelphia, PA
(215) 963-6000
(interactive-shopping technology)

QVC Network, Inc.
Westchester, PA
(215) 430-1000
(television-shopping network)

Home Shopping Club, Inc.
St. Petersburg, FL
(813) 572-8585
(television-shopping network)

Jupiter Communications Company
New York, NY
(212) 941-9252
(consulting in online information services)

National Infomercial Marketing
Association
Washington, DC
(202) 962-8342
(industry association of individuals and companies producing infomercials)

Cabletelevision Advertising Bureau
New York, NY
(212) 751-7770
(industry association of businesses in cable TV ad sales, production, and systems management)

TV Macy's
New York, NY
(212) 560-1779
(television-shopping programming)

Arcades

The arcade amusement business has benefited from recent changes in the American scene. The number of children has grown, and poor economic conditions have pushed more families to find inexpensive forms of entertainment. One result: many traditional arcades are now called "family entertainment centers."

Arcade standards such as pinball and miniature kiddie rides are still popular, but new technology and consumer interests are affecting what arcades have to offer. One of the biggest growth areas is redemption games, interactive games that issue coupons redeemable for a range of toys, plush animals, tools, housewares, jewelry, and other items.

Due to this trend, one of the oldest arcade games in America is getting new attention. Skee Ball, invented in 1907 by the Philadelphia Toboggin Company, is now an industry leader in the redemption arena.

Based on mechanical action, Skee Ball is competing with a slew of new electronic games such as Neck-N-Neck, a video horse race. Other redemption games attracting renewed interest are a new generation of "coin pushers," ball skill devices, and arcade versions of popular games such as "Hungry, Hungry Hippos," first released as a home game for children.

Redemption games have captured up to half of games at some arcades and are now moving into new arenas. Fast-food restaurants will probably be one of the new venues, as will strip malls and airports, because some new redemption games are self-contained, with the prizes included in such free-standing units.

While some amusement games are going solo, the general theme for arcades is "bigger is better." Centers are enlarging their floor space to accommodate more games, devices, and customers. Some are even adding rides. The Mall of America in Minnesota pushes this concept to an extreme. Its arcade is a full-sized amusement park.

Arcade machines have progressed from mechanical pinballs to interactive electronic video games, but the most futuristic technology of all, virtual reality, is still in its infancy. This computer-based technology has become the "darling" of the amusement business in less than two years, producing profits even before widespread applications have been developed for other industries, including science and medicine.

The technology involves computer-simulated effects into which the position of a user's hands, head, or body is projected, allowing the sensation of navigating through artificial realities, manipulating artificial objects, or fighting against computer-generated foes.

In the amusement industry, virtual-reality applications are led by W Industry's Virtuality machines, with 120 units in operation in the U.S. as of mid-1993. Extremely strong consumer reaction to these futuristic game devices has prompted a virtual rush of investment and development by other companies eager to cash in on the trend.

Developments that will affect the high-tech arcade business in the next few years include higher resolution graphics, greater detail and realism, and more variety for virtual reality games; more simulators based on military and commercial flight equipment; and improved computer-generated human figures for interactive games. SimGraphics is developing the Vactor Animation Creation System (VACS), which will use computer-generated characters whose motion and reactions are developed from real actors performing real-time movement. Interactive entertainment based on these characters will permit realistic reactions between players and virtual actors, including "morphing," transforming one character into another through computerized alteration.

RESOURCES:

International Association
of Amusement Parks
and Attractions
Alexandria, VA
(703) 836-4800
(industry association of
manufacturers and operators of
amusement parks and related
facilities)

Amusement and Music
Operators Association
Chicago, IL
(312) 245-1021
(industry association of businesses
involved with coin-operated games)

Game Manufacturers Association
Grinnell, IA
(515) 236-5027
(industry association for
manufacturers and distributors of
commercial games)

Coastal Amusement Distributors
Lakewood, NJ
(908) 905-6662
(supplier of redemption games)

Namco-America
Santa Clara, CA
(408) 383-3900
(amusement game and redemption-
machine manufacturers)

Amtronics, Inc.
Metairie, LA
(504) 831-0691
(computer imaging services)

Capcom USA, Inc.
Santa Clara, CA
(408) 727-0400
(computer games)

Skee Ball, Inc
Chalfont, PA
(215) 997-8900
(coin-operated games)

Magic Edge, Inc.
Mountain View, CA
(415) 965-8819
(flight simulators for entertainment applications)

V-Space
Boulder, CO
(303) 440-0442
(virtual-reality arcade operations and virtual-reality consulting)

Movies

The recent popularity of violence in movies may be abating, although not because of legislation. Cyclical movements usually change on their own—as much from oversaturation and consumer boredom as anything else. This trend has another cause—children. Baby boomers having babies, the so-called "echo baby boom," are transforming the adult-oriented society of the past two decades into a new child-centered universe, with an obvious impact on the popularity of family-oriented films.

In the early 1990s, the family-oriented theme began to erode the prevalence of violence and sexuality at the box office. Hollywood is pumping out a new generation of films geared to a more traditional theater audience. This trend will intensify in the next few years, with some inevitable consequences.

Directions ripe for profitability include more animation, animal films, child stars, and marketing tie-ins with comic-strip characters. Within a few years, the trend could reach a point of outright exploitation, cloning, and gimmicks. Expect a big-screen debut for Barney; low-quality animated features; and a new rash of a perennial Hollywood gimmick, 3-D.

Walt Disney Pictures is positioned to profit most from this trend, although the market appetite is certain to be larger than Disney alone can accommodate. Other new players in the market include Nickelodeon, the cable-television channel for children, in a production collaboration with Twentieth Century Fox. Universal Pictures, Fox, and Time Warner are also actively expanding their development and production of family films.

RESOURCES:

Motion Picture Association
of America
Washington, DC
(202) 293-1966
(industry association of producers
and distributors of motion pictures)

Other Movie Trends

MODERN SOUND While many movie goers have cut down on theater attendance because of the influence of videocassettes at home and the rising cost of movie tickets, few home-viewing systems can match the quality or image size of even a small movie theater. Even this difference, however, is losing is effectiveness in luring people away from TV, except for major blockbusters or movies with highly marketed special effects. Videocassette rentals and sales have boomed, despite relatively low reproduction quality. Viewers seem unimpressed by what they are missing. Television sets, however, are gradually improving image quality.

The movie industry is attempting to combat these trends by adding viewing value to the theater experience, especially with improvements in sound systems. A modern, sophisticated sound system in a theater setting greatly enhances the visual experience. But the expense of installing the digital reproduction equipment that provides this auditory effect in individual theaters is high—up to $20,000. At present, the industry does not follow a digital sound standard. Its solution is to print different versions of a film with sound tracks coded for the different standards. The initial players in this field include Sony, with Sony Dynamic Digital Sound (SDDS); and Dolby, with Dolby Stereo Digital. MCA, with Digital Theater System (DTS), is a new arrival with the advantage of being the lowest-priced system to date.

RESOURCES:

Dolby Laboratories, Inc.
San Francisco, CA
(415) 558-0200
(noise reduction and signal
processing technology)

MCA, Inc.
Universal City, CA
(818) 777-1000
(theatrical music reproduction
systems)

LOCATION LOGIC Filmmakers have recently been increasingly driven to select locations based on financial considerations rather than editorial choice. Cities and countries are often willing to bend the rules and offer monetary concessions in order to attract filmmakers, but two factors may offer new competition. First, countries in the former Soviet Union are turning out to be excellent low-cost options for many types of films. Two, the biggest cost impediment most movie productions

1994 Movies

Movies in production that will be released in late 1993 or 1994 include (starring roles are subject to change and production politics can delay release schedules):

Bad Girls, a western version of *Thelma and Louise,* starring Andie MacDowell, Mary Stuart Masterson, Drew Barrymore, and Madeline Stowe

Broken Dreams, starring River Phoenix and Winona Ryder

Carmen Sandiego, a live-action feature based on the character in the best-selling education computer software

Cats, animated version of the Broadway musical from Steven Spielberg

The Client, starring Susan Sarandon and Tommy Lee Jones

The Color of Knight, starring Bruce Willis

Cowboy Way, starring Woody Harrelson

Crooklyn, N.Y., directed by Spike Lee

Curious George, an animated feature starring the famous monkey of children's literature

Dead Sleep, starring Demi Moore

Fair Game, starring Sylvester Stallone

The Flintstones, live-action version of the animated TV series, starring Elizabeth Taylor, John Goodman, and Rick Moranis

A Good Man in Africa, starring Sean Connery and Joanne Whelley-Kilmer

Greed, starring Michael J. Fox

The Immortals, starring Sharon Stone

Inspector Gadget, a live-action feature based on the television character

Intersection, starring Sharon Stone, Richard Gere, and Lolita Davidovich

It's Pat, the Movie, a feature based on the character created by Julia Sweeney on "Saturday Night Live"

Joe's Apartment, a feature based on an MTV short subject, starring thousands of cockroaches

Jungle Book, a Walt Disney live-action feature remake of the animated version

The Last of the Dog Men, starring Tom Berenger

Lightning Jack, starring Paul Hogan

Maverick, a remake of the original, starring Mel Gibson and Paul Newman, with James Garner, the original Maverick, in a cameo role

Mistress of the Seas, a big-budget swashbuckler based on the infamous female pirates Anne Bonnie and Mary Reed, starring Geena Davis

The Muppet Treasure Island, the next Muppet adventure from Jim Henson Productions

My Girl 2, the sequel, starring Macaulay Culkin

On Deadly Ground, the directoral debut of Steven Seagal, starring Michael Caine

The Pagemaster, animated/live-action feature starring Macaulay Culkin

The Paper, starring Glenn Close and Michael Keaton

Pocahontas, a full-length animated feature from Walt Disney

The Quick and the Dead, starring Sharon Stone

The Ref, starring Judy Davis

The Royal Way, starring Bob Hoskins and Kiefer Sutherland

Serial Mom, starring Kathleen Turner

The Shadow, a feature based on the adventures of the radio character, starring Alec Baldwin

Swan Lake, animated feature with the voice of John Cleese

Time Cop, starring Jean-Claude Van Damme

Tollbooth, starring Louise Fletcher and Lawrence Tierney

Tombstone, another remake of the famous gunfight at the OK corral, starring Kurt Russell and Val Kilmer

Total Recall II, the sequel, starring Arnold Schwarzenegger

True Lies, starring Arnold Schwarzenegger

Wyatt Earp, another remake of the life of the infamous lawman, including yet another recreation of the gunfight at the OK corral, starring Kevin Costner and Dennis Quaid

ENTERTAINMENT AND THE MEDIA

face in the U.S.—union-based rules and fees—is beginning to crumble, as more unions in large cities such as New York and Los Angeles adopt more flexible policies, including deferring extra expenses until a film has been released and is generating cash flow.

SMALL-SCREEN PREVIEWS An ambitious new venture is developing a way for television viewers to see some new movie releases at the same time they hit theaters. Tele-Communications, Inc. and Carolco Pictures, Inc. will offer this service using pay-per-view options in some cable systems.

RESOURCES:

Tele-Communications, Inc.
Englewood, CO
(303) 267-5500
(cable-television services)

Music

INTERACTIVE ROCK AND ROLL Pushing the edge of experimentation in rock music, some musicians are producing compact disc products that offer listeners the opportunity to interact with the traditionally static listening experience, including David Bowie, Billy Idol, Edgar Winter, Thomas Dolby, Prince, U2, Michael Jackson, Madonna, and Todd Rundgren. Multimedia discs combine film or video clips, graphic art, text, and music so users can explore historical backgrounds, notes, recording-session experiences, or other audio and visual elements of the rock scene. With interactive compositions, users can play along or assemble new tunes from the available components, a sort of "desktop karaoke."

At the most advanced level, interactive rock discs will expand the concept of composer to allow a new kind of proactive listening. Users can alter the style and mood of a piece, not just mechanical components such as tempo or key. Some interactive discs will also provide an educational function, by allowing musical selections to be played one part at a time, isolating vocals or instrumental parts from other elements.

The interactive rock movement is just beginning to blossom, but could grow rapidly as more consumers purchase multimedia players, CD-I machines, and other formats that support interactive technology. No single interactive format yet dominates the industry, complicating production and marketing decisions. Consumers, however, may solve the problem, by responding enthusiastically to the celebrity status of rock music and making decisions about interactive computers that they have not made with the prevailing choice of interactive products— mostly games, reference, and educational material.

RESOURCES:

Recording Industry Association
of America
Washington, DC
(202) 775-0101
(industry association of
manufacturers of sound recordings)

Independent Music Association
Ringwood, NJ
(201) 831-1317
(industry association of musicians,
composers, and independent
record-label companies)

ENTERTAINMENT
AND THE MEDIA

Other Musical Trends

DO-IT-YOURSELF CDS With the spread of compact-disc technology comes a new era in home recording, rapidly making cassette-tape recording obsolete among many garage bands, neighborhood musical groups, and other amateur ventures. Numerous commercial services now offer CD replication for fixed rates. Musicians provide a master recording tape and receive a set number of CDs in exchange. Costs range from $200 to $300 at the low end for an original CD master, and $2 to $3 for each duplicate disc. Some services provide package deals: $2,000 to $3,000, for instance, for 500 CDs and 500 traditional cassette tapes. These services will allow more startup bands, experimental groups, and "noncommercial" creators to put products on the market.

ONLINE DEMOS Intrepid musicians and hackers are creating music "demos" on online computer services. The demos use music, animation, graphics, and text in a freeform development that *Boardwatch* magazine calls "the data version of Music Videos." Often developed in multi-person collaboration at separate sites, with one person adding to the work of another, demos are an exploratory form of music linked with computerized technology. The trend is reportedly more established in Europe.

DIGITAL SOUND EFFECTS The spreading popularity of digital synthesizers, electronic musical instruments, and computer-controlled musical production has also increased the demand for preproduced samples, sound effects, voice effects, and musical "sound bites" with which desktop users can create new productions. Aided by the decreased costs of reproducing music on CDs (see above), many independent producers are assembling sound-effects collections on CDs and marketing them to this new home-based industry. Collections range from drum effects created by professional drummers to traditional movie sound effects. Some digital sound producers also offer these "albums" in various floppy disk formats.

SECOND-HAND CDS Long-lived compact discs are now developing a hot secondary market. Outlets specializing in the purchase and resale of used CDs have existed in most major cities since CDs first entered commercial distribution, but most have been small, independent facilities with local markets. Now big stores and chains are entering the picture. In 1992, 407 million new CDs were sold in the U.S., a figure expected to increase by at least 5 percent in 1993 and 1994. In the used-disc market, the going price for albums is about half the cost of new releases. Because people who buy used discs are less likely to buy new ones, music companies oppose this trend. So far, most of the opposition has come in the form of real or threatened withdrawal of cooperative advertising funds for individual stores.

PROTECTED MERCHANDISE Following a 1993 decision to adopt a single anti-theft system, most of the 14,000 music stores in the U.S. are expected to have a new system in place by mid-1994. Developed by Sensormatic Electronic Corporation, the new shoplifting detectors rely on acousto-magnetic sensors imbedded in tags on compact disc boxes. The shift to an industry-wide system was prompted by efforts to end the use of "long boxes," excess packaging formerly used to merchandise (and deter theft of) CDs.

MUSICAL MORES Growing minority populations and increasing ethnic pride are boosting the popularity of new types of ethnic music. In California, several styles of traditional Mexican music have evolved into hot new sounds, including banda, ranchera, and texano. Salsa, popular in mainstream circles in the 1950s, is now on the comeback trail, attracting audiences outside of traditional Hispanic communities. The salsa upswing includes the rediscovery of noted salsa artists, reissues of classic albums, and salsa-inspired tunes crossing over into country and rock formats.

RESOURCES:

Disc Makers
Philadelphia, PA
(800) 468-9353
(CD mastering and reproduction)

E-mu Systems, Inc.
Scotts Valley, CA
(408) 438-1921
(music synthesizers)

Sensormatic Electronic Corporation
Deerfield Beach, FL
(305) 427-9700
(retail loss-prevention systems)

Hollywood Edge
Hollywood, CA
(213) 466-6523
(sound-effects recordings)

National Association of
Recording Merchandisers
Marlton, NJ
(609) 596-2221
(industry association of recorded-
entertainment-product retailers)

Keyboard
published by Miller Freeman, Inc.
San Francisco, CA
(415) 905-2200
(keyboard-based music publication)

CD-ROM Professional
published by Pemberton Press, Inc.
Wilton, CT
(203) 761-1466
(practical how-to information on
CD-ROM use and publishing)

Boardwatch
Littleton, CO
(303) 973-6038
(online systems and computer-
bulletin-board systems publication)

Book Trends

The book industry continues to demonstrate the growing power of baby-boomer bucks. Its annual growth now outpaces many other consumer product categories. Maturing boomers are buying books at a record rate and should continue to do so for the next few decades.

The nature of the industry, however, is changing gradually over time, moving away from an era of few very profitable "big books" and into a period marked by more diverse success. From small presses to major publishing houses, there are more titles earning profits. This is happening because publishers are paying more attention to marketing and taking greater care in choosing titles to publish in the first place.

At the same time, computerized ordering systems are beginning to dominate the bookselling end of the business. Computerized ordering, the book industry's version of "just-in-time" stocking, allows more bookstores to order titles only as they need them, avoiding large stocks of unsellable merchandise that end up returned to the publisher.

In the initial stage of electronic ordering, booksellers were able to connect to wholesalers and distributors. The second phase of this system, direct connections between booksellers and publishers, is now beginning to develop. Major publishing houses such as Random House, HarperCollins, and Simon & Schuster now provide electronic links to retailers.

Some publishers are also applying the just-in-time principle to the printing process, using electronic links to speed up the production of reprints and tailor printing runs to actual orders. Reprint orders can now be processed in less than one week. Ten years ago average turnaround was six weeks.

While these modern practices speed up and automate the distribution of books, the "old-fashioned" sales connection, the sales representative, may have to evolve to survive. Sales reps no longer directly account for as many sales to bookstores as they have in the past, especially for larger publishers. But with so many titles from which to choose, the average bookstore still needs guidance, suggestions, and support from sales reps to make sense of the publishing jungle.

The new sales rep may provide more service and information support and process fewer orders. At some large publishers, including Random House, the change is already in motion. Its sales reps make fewer personal calls to accounts, staying in touch via telephone and fax. New personalized telephone reps handle smaller accounts and regions with widely dispersed bookstores.

These developments are gradually turning the book industry from a business run by creative license to one at least influenced, if not led, by pragmatic business decisions. This may reduce some of the over-replicated shallowness that has characterized the industry's nonfiction output for many years. An informal study of current and upcoming business titles, for instance, shows that the breadth of subjects is widening, fewer copycat titles are in evidence, and more publishers are willing to promote substantive topics over faddish subjects.

BUSINESS BOOKS Already a well-respected and profitable area of publishing, business books may enjoy even greater success through the remainder of the decade because of the expected influence of baby boomers. Hitting their professional peaks, baby boomers are fueling much of the current vitality in ongoing education, advanced studies, and second careers, all of which can be addressed by books. Technological impacts, changes in government regulations, and new methods of marketing and research put even the average careerist in need of constant new information. Not only will business books benefit from the increasing demand for information and guidance in these areas, they will direct the path some of these trends may take.

In turn, technology is affecting the way business books themselves are created and formatted. Businesses are avid users and developers of programs, systems, and data. The result will be the first practical books in computer-readable format. Business titles naturally lend themselves to the electronic environment more than most fiction or other nonfiction titles. Combination book and disk editions are called "hybrids" (this book is one of them).

As far as subject matter goes, American business people have diminishing interest in books about the Japanese approach to management and manufacturing due to overhype, overselling, and the diminishing economic strength of that country. Domestic solutions to American business problems replaces that interest, particularly more focused, specialized topics. Fueled by the approach of the new millennium, the recent power shift in Washington, and the anticipated effects of global policies and entities like the North American Free Trade Agreement and the European Economic Community, more books will offer explanations and philosophical advice about economic theory.

RESOURCES:

Baker & Taylor Books
Charlotte, NC
(704) 357-3500
(book wholesaler)

Ingram Book Company
LaVergne, TN
(615) 793-5000
(book wholesaler)

American Booksellers Association
Tarrytown, NY
(914) 631-7800
(industry association of retailers and wholesalers in the book trade)

Other Book Trends

SUPERSTORES In less than ten years, the number of large independent bookstores has grown from only a few to almost 200 in 1993. These superstores have developed and thrived in the major book markets, large coastal cities, and a few large inland cities such as Chicago and Denver. In the past few years, their success—annual sales of $1 million per store are common—has attracted competition from both established bookstore chains and outside investors. While projections for growth in the bookselling market are healthy because of the baby boom, some markets may already be saturated with superstores. In the next few years, increased competition is likely to result in failure for some franchised outlets and independents. Because of the added value that independents provide through customer service, some industry insiders expect that Barnes & Noble superstores will lose out, because they are competing with reduced service.

TECHNOLOGICAL INTERPRETATIONS Science and technology subjects will increasingly offer introductory and explanatory texts for the curious reading public, those who are interested but do not have the background to understand technical discussions. These mainstream science guides range from astronomy to bioengineering.

MIDLIFE CRISIS The aging of the baby boom will result in at least one hot topic for books: menopause. These books will carry descriptive information, research results, self-help advice, professional guidance, and anthropological and historical perspectives. A few will also talk to men, explaining the effects of menopause on spouses as well as their own psychological if not physical mid-life transition.

MAINSTREAM FEMINISM With the exception of a few recent bestsellers dealing with gender issues from a feminist perspective, most recent books in the area have been published by small presses and distributed more as specialty books than mainstream titles. The latest trend for these books in large publishing houses is to downplay traditional feminist politics in favor of content with broader appeal, including historic perspectives, anthropology, politics, and mainstream culture.

MULTICULTURAL FASHION Interest in multiculturalism will continue, with less emphasis on political correctness and more on recognized cultural talents. Both fiction and nonfiction books are benefiting from this movement, as publishers seek serious, substantive works. In this phase, titles by ethnic and cultural minorities are finding expanding audiences within their own communities—black writers appealing to blacks, Hispanic writers appealing to Hispanics—rather than the largely white audiences of the past.

At the same time, the majority white audience is benefiting from a wider range of authentic voices not previously available to them. In turn, the market and appreciation for disparate cultures will likely spawn a renaissance in many nonmainstream American communities, producing more works by and for increasingly distinct niches and sub-communities. This may become most evident among native Americans, who are often lumped together. Distinct literary voices will emerge from varied tribal traditions. Even the mainstream Euro-centrist population will be part of this trend, with more books discussing the history and cultural heritage of groups from various countries and religious backgrounds in "the old country."

AUDIO DISCOUNTS Healthy growth in the books-on-tape market has led to a new niche: low-cost products. Much of the market has focused on rental tapes as a commuting perk for book readers who drive their own cars—mostly bestsellers. The new trend parallels the paperback concept, with lower prices, condensed versions, and less costly packaging. The growing market for books-on-tape will also affect how they are sold; more tapes will be distributed through nonbookstore outlets, including drugstores, convenience stores, and supermarkets.

BOOKS ON TV Several new book-related ventures are coming to the small screen. "First Edition," a weekly PBS venture, will feature interviews with noted authors. Booknet, a 24-hour cable channel, will feature interviews, reviews, and industry news. (See also "Cable Clutter," page 154.)

RESOURCES:

First Edition
New York, NY
(212) 243-4400
(television show about books)

Booknet
New York, NY
(212) 698-7808
(television channel about books)

Books of the Future

Although it is still too early to determine what forms future books may take, it is increasingly evident that some already created forms will survive. Electronic book formats now include floppy disks, CD-ROMs, CD-I (compact disc interactive), and online.

In most of these guises, the basic nature of the traditional book survives. Only the display changes, from type on paper to characters on a video screen. But this format adds nothing to the value of a manuscript. In fact, it usually detracts from the more eye-pleasing and inexpensive method of reading text on printed pages. Only electronic books with "added value" can expect to find an appreciative audience. These will include reference books, catalogs, dictionaries, and some textbooks. It excludes most fiction, popular nonfiction, and other casual reading material.

Added value in an electronic book includes finding information and linking subjects, tasks for which computer power is well-suited. Most text and data may need no more assistance than this, although graphic images, sound, and motion may add a further benefit for some applications.

ENTERTAINMENT AND THE MEDIA

Most current electronic books are available on CD-ROM, such as Compton's Multimedia Encyclopedia. Production of these types of multimedia titles is on a rapid rise; more titles will be available over the next few years at a lower average price. But most have so far demonstrated little advantage over "old-fashioned" print titles. The next generation of discs will hopefully make up for many of these deficiencies.

Books may also become available on online services such as the Internet. As a first step, various ventures are underway to link customers with books for sale. United Techbook, a technical book company, offers more than 10,000 titles through an online catalog, complete with annotated entries for subject searching. Some online library services also plan to add ordering capabilities to their menus. Because these ventures have the potential to create disharmonious relations with retail booksellers, they are likely to be confined to academic and scholarly texts, traditionally underrepresented in bookstores.

RESOURCES:

Brock and Associates
Denver, CO
(303) 333-2772
(consulting for books, CD-ROMs)

Texas Internet Consulting
Austin, TX
(512) 451-6176
(consulting for computer networks and the Internet)

Software Tool & Die
Brookline, MA
(617) 739-0202
(online bookstore accessible on the Internet for full text and book ordering)

CARL Systems
Denver, CO
(303) 758-3030
(online library and information services)

United Techbook
Boulder, CO
(303) 443-7037
(online technical book ordering)

Johnson Books
Boulder, CO
(303) 443-1576
(production and publishing of books and catalogues on CD-ROM)

Magazines with a Future

As with television, the magazine industry has been talking about the impending arrival of interactive magazines, electronic versions of traditional printed publications. In this industry, however, the recession of the early 1990s has reduced advertising revenue for magazines, as recessions typically do. There is a growing sense among some periodical professionals that magazines will not recover this time and that they are not capable of surviving competition from other media, changing demographics, and new technology.

Depressed revenue has not been universal, however. Some periodicals are finding fresh energy and expansion as American society heads into the last few years of the millennium. Current trends in the magazine industry include:

VALUE CONSCIOUSNESS Consumers are less interested in lavish lifestyles and extravagant spending. The new focus has shifted to "affordable luxuries," including do-it-yourself projects that add elegance on a budget, nature-oriented outdoor activities, improving physical and mental well-being, adding meaning to the aging process, creating new businesses, and working independently.

ELECTRONIC ISSUES Some magazines have already produced compact-disc versions combining graphics, moving images, text, and sound. Players experimenting with this format include *Newsweek, Time, Cosmopolitan*, and *Audubon*. Projects reportedly underway include discs from *Bon Appetit* and *Reader's Digest*.

In addition to versions on discs, some consumer magazines have taken the first steps in providing online access to their publications, only with a twist. Although the text of published magazine articles has been available for many years through services such as Dialog, these new online magazines will allow readers to interact with the material instead of just looking at it. These new versions will provide a range of interactive capabilities for readers, including e-mail links to editorial staff, user-participation forums, surveys, and product databases. Titles reportedly going online within a few years include *The New Republic, New York, National Review, Penthouse, PC Magazine,* and *Home Office Computing.*

Many consumer publications with online editions or plans to develop them will go online with existing commercial services, including Prodigy, Compuserve, and America Online. Some magazines, however, have set up their own online connections, capturing payments through credit cards or "900" telephone fees. Apple Computer, too, is exploring online futures for magazines through a design laboratory where a critical aspect of new electronic formats must be developed: advertising support.

RESOURCES:

Apple Design Lab
Boulder, CO
(303) 444-2204
(research and development for
advertising-supported online
magazines)

Magazine Publishers of America
New York, NY
(212) 752-0055
(industry association of
magazine publishers)

Newsweek
published by Newsweek, Inc.
New York, NY
(212) 350-4000

Time
published by Time, Inc.
New York, NY
(212) 586-1212

Cosmopolitan
published by The Hearst
Corporation
New York, NY
(212) 649-2000

Audubon
published by the National Audubon
Society
New York, NY
(212) 979-3000

The New Republic
published by The New Republic,
Inc.
Washington, DC
(202) 331-7494

New York
published by K-III magazines
New York, NY
(212) 447-4700

National Review
published by National Review, Inc.
New York, NY
(212) 679-7330

Penthouse
published by General Media
International, Ltd.
New York, NY
(212) 496-6100

PC Magazine
published by Ziff-Davis Publishing
Company
New York, NY
(212) 503-5100

Home Office Computing
published by Scholastic, Inc.
New York, NY
(212) 343-6100

Newspapers of the Future

Various projects are underway to develop future concepts for newspapers. Knight-Ridder, Inc. is using a design laboratory for its venture. The Media Laboratory at the Massachusetts Institute of Technology is examining how to individualize newspapers electronically. Gannett, publisher of *USA Today*, uses its Advanced Systems Lab to research new technology and its application to newspapers.

All of these projects focus on the eventual widespread use of electronic connections such as interactive television, telephone-information delivery, and wireless data broadcasts to handheld computers. In the meantime, other technologies are already providing new venues for traditional newspaper content. Of these, fax publishing and direct response have achieved the greatest inroads. (See also "Fax Publishing," page 186.)

Prodigy Services and Cox Newspapers are developing an online network to deliver news, scheduled for startup in limited markets at the end of 1993. America Online is also expanding to offer digital news through the development of an electronic edition of the *Chicago Tri-*

bune, one of the investors in this network. As most homes do not have fax machines or computers, these services are most likely to find acceptance in the office environment. National and local newspapers should find increasing interest in the business community, particularly with customized searching and targeted information.

But virtually everyone does have a telephone, and many newspapers have seen healthy profits by adapting 900 telephone services to offer up-to-the-minute headlines, sports scores, weather information, and classified ads. Future expansion is expected to diminish, however, because of a limited market—such calls are routinely blocked in hotels and offices—and competition from other, free sources of the same information. In order to maintain interest, newspapers will be forced to shift to free phone services, adding promotional and advertising tracks to cover their costs. One exception: personal ads.

The full-fledged electronic newspaper of the future may be years away, but information junkies already access several services that provide some news electronically. These specialized news-delivery services make use of existing technologies and, for a fee, keep customers informed of what is going on. Examples include Motorola, which uses its EMBARC wireless e-mail service to deliver news and weather reports to portable computers. The National Dispatch Center delivers news items to customers of its paging services. The NewsMaster/Front Page service includes business reports, sports, and weather, as well as puzzles and trivia. BellSouth Corporation and Pacific Telesis Group in Los Angeles are testing news services for cellular-phone users. McCaw Cellular Communications, the largest cellular-phone company, is also reportedly developing news broadcasts for its customers.

A final move toward the paperless dimension in the newspaper industry is an experiment with electronic advertiser billing. In 1993, several daily papers and two national retail accounts—Dillard Department Stores and Sears, Roebuck & Company—began testing direct electronic links to order and pay for display advertising, a program known as Multimarket Advertiser Product (MAP).

RESOURCES:

Newspaper Association of America
Reston, VA
(703) 648-1000
(industry association of newspaper
owners and operators)

The Media Laboratory, MIT
Cambridge, MA
(617) 253-0300
(research and development for
electronic media)

Knight-Ridder Information
Design Lab
Boulder, CO
(303) 443-3312
(research and development for the
newspaper of the future)

Gannet Company, Inc.
Arlington, VA
(703) 284-6000
(newspaper publishing)

Cleveland Today
Cleveland, OH
(216) 344-3200
(fax publishing sample)

JournalFax
(800) 759-9966
(Wall Street Journal fax publishing
sample)

Prodigy Services Company
White Plains, NY
(914) 993-8000
(online information service)

Cox Newspapers, Inc.
Atlanta, GA
(404) 843-5000
(newspaper publishing)

Tribune Newspaper Company
Chicago, IL
(312) 222-3232
(newspaper publishing)

National Dispatch Center, Inc.
San Diego, CA
(619) 481-9500
(paging and communications
services)

BellSouth Corporation
Atlanta, GA
(404) 249-2000
(telephone services)

Pacific Telesis Group
San Francisco, CA
(415) 394-3000
(telephone services)

McCaw Cellular
Communications, Inc.
Kirkland, WA
(206) 827-4500
(cellular-telephone services)

ENTERTAINMENT
AND THE MEDIA

Fax Publishing

The 1993 Gallup/Pitney Bowes Fax Usage and Applications Study of Fortune 500 companies revealed a 40 percent increase in facsimile use in just one year. The number of fax machines in these companies grew 25 percent between 1992 and 1993. At the opposite end of the spectrum, however, home offices have yet to take to fax technology in a big way. A survey of this segment by BIS Strategic Decisions indicated that only 5 percent of an estimated 34 million home offices had fax machines in 1991. Lower prices, more sales outlets, and an increasing need to make connections via fax are all working to change this situation. By the end of 1994, fax penetration of the home-office market is expected to double.

As fax use continues to boom at all levels, fax publishing also gains popularity. In fact, fax publishing has now become an established service in many businesses. Can fax publishing be considered a new member of the media family? This, in fact, may gradually be happening as commercially available applications continue to expand and more uses are found for this electronic format.

Developments in Fax Publishing

PRESS FAX Many newspapers have adopted fax services to provide readers with up-to-date information, including news, stock reports, classified ads, automobile reviews, mortgage information, tax forms, and advertising. These services, at least so far, have been developing as appendages to the regular newspaper format, offered as fee-based or free services to readers and subscribers. In some cases, added value includes custom reports and reprinted material. (See "Newspapers of the Future," page 183.)

CUSTOMIZED READER SERVICE "Bingo cards"—the magazine feature that allows readers to circle numbers on mail-in cards to request more information about advertisers or articles—have been increasingly replaced by fax features that allow instant response. Some problems have arisen from this new service. Publishers and companies soliciting responses are not always prepared to fulfill readers' requests as quickly as they arrive.

DIRECT RESPONSE Direct response is a specialized form of fax publishing that connects customers, potential customers, and suppliers. It uses automated telephone voice menus, with which a caller specifies what they want—product specifications, prices, descriptions—by punching the number keys on the telephone in response to menu prompts. Information is then automatically faxed to the caller. Direct response is spreading rapidly and may soon become the dominant form of fax publishing. It has clear advantages: familiarity with the equipment, low overhead costs, instant response, and the ability to "capture" customer and demographic information. Variations of direct response are now in use in the realms of newspapers (*The Wall Street Journal*), personal computers (Intel), health (The National Cancer Institute), and government (state of California business tax forms). Complete units for running direct-response operations can cost less than $5,000, and leasing options are increasingly available. Costs to the customer range from free—usually through "800" telephone numbers—to moderate, with per-minute or per-page connect charges paid by check, credit card, or "900" telephone charges.

FAX NETWORK Experiments are underway to develop alternative distribution systems for fax messaging, using the Internet network to avoid the costs and bottlenecks found on ordinary long-distance telephone lines. (See pages 26 and 91 for more on Internet.) This project will allow local users to transmit faxes to "cell sites" where built-in codes would send the fax via an Internet connection to another cell site, where it would be retransmitted in fax form to its intended addressee. This type of transmission should also allow virtually complete messaging between e-mail addresses and fax numbers. The service is now in use in Washington, D.C., areas of California, and the University of Michigan.

ENTERTAINMENT AND THE MEDIA

RESOURCES:

American Facsimile Association
Philadelphia, PA
(215) 963-9110
(national organization providing
fax information, subsidiary of
U.S. Fax, Inc.)

FaxBack, Inc.
Beaverton, OR
(503) 645-1114
(automated fax services)

Pitney Bowes, Inc.
Stamford, CT
(203) 356-5000
(mailing and fax systems)

CancerFax
(301) 402-5874
(specialized fax publisher)

Internet fax service
E-mail to:
TPC-FAQ@TOWN.HALL.ORG.

BIS Strategic Decisions, Inc.
(617) 982-9500
(industrial research and consulting)

JOBS
AND EDUCATION

JOBS AND EDUCATION

Entrepreneurship will be on the rise in 1994, due to corporate downsizing and technology that makes small businesses powerful competitors. Training is one of the year's major trends, with professionals and tradesmen seeking accreditation from an increasing number of organizations, and schools and community colleges providing customized employee education.

Entrepreneurial Fever

A combination of factors is turning more Americans into freelance entrepreneurs, deserting the security of weekly paychecks for the uncertain territory of self-employment. As the decade rolls on, this trend could accelerate into a boom. What is driving more adults into independent ventures instead of traditional careers or mainstream employment?

■ **Tradition** Business culture in the United States has always celebrated self-employment. American business history emphasizes the success of the "self-made man," fortunes generated by ingenuity, and the satisfaction of working independently of bosses and time clocks.

■ **The economy** The recession of the early 1990s and generally sluggish economy is driving many workers to become pessimists about employment security. Many have been directly affected—they've been laid off.

■ **Generational cycles** The gradually aging characteristic of the population, mostly influenced by the entry of one-third of the population—baby boomers—into middle age, is prompting many workers to look for other satisfactions than those found on a payroll or in a traditional career.

■ **Conformity** What neighbors and peers are doing can have a profound effect on individuals. From car models to lawn ornaments, this type of conformity is a powerful force. When the trend is for more people to work for themselves, it can gain momentum just because of the tendency for people to follow others' examples.

■ **Funds** Generally speaking, people beginning new ventures in their 40s and 50s have more money or access to credit than younger adults. Professional workers who have been laid off or are facing early retirement because of downsizing also often receive separation packages or lump sums that help them start new businesses. Recent signs indicate that banks and other financial institutions are warming up to a new cycle of small-business lending. In 1992, after five consecutive years of decline, the number of new-business incorporations increased by 7 percent.

■ **Technology** New technology includes cheaper and more powerful computers, software, and development tools such as expert systems and CAD/CAM programs. These, plus the increased availability of information and data, allow more individuals to be in business for themselves as part of the modern era of product manufacturing and services.

■ **Military technology overflow** With widespread layoffs in the military-industrial sector, many experienced, creative technical experts are being loosed into the private sector. Since relatively few openings exist for these workers and because many are affected by the above factors, the military's loss could become an entrepreneurial gain.

RESOURCES:

National Federation of Independent Business
Washington, DC
(202) 554-9000
(association of businesses from most commercial sectors)

Entrepreneurship Institute
Columbus, OH
(614) 895-1153
(national organization assisting in the development and creation of businesses)

HOME ALONE

Projected growth in employment for self-employed workers in occupations with 50,000 or more workers, 1990-2005.

occupation	number of jobs gained 1990-2005	percent change
Executive, administrative, and managerial	508,000	32%
Service (including cleaning, food preparation, barbers, child care, etc.)	442,000	36
Professional specialties (lawyers, doctors, writers, social scientists, designers, etc.)	281,000	19
Precision production, craft, and repair	246,000	15
Marketing and sales	72,000	4
Administrative support, including clerical	44,000	13
Technicians and related support	25,000	23
Operators, fabricators, and laborers	15,000	3
Agriculture, forestry, fishing, and related	-131,000	-10

Source: Outlook: 1990-2005: Occupational Employment, *Bureau of Labor Statistics, May 1992*

Learning to Earn

A new fervor for professional credentials is beginning to emerge. From dog catchers to middle managers, many careers are affected by this urge to create appropriate qualifications, training, and accreditation in fields not now covered. For highly trained professions such as medicine, accreditation has long been standard. Now the benefits of such systems are being applied to other professions.

Accreditation usually includes advanced training and testing. Many employment specialties are now creating accreditation standards that involve job skills such as computer use, interpersonal communications, quality issues, and government-driven work changes such as safety, access for those with disabilities, and environmental standards.

The new accreditation trend is rooted in the drive to produce better workers and improve efficiency, performance, and service. Many companies are participating, if not driving, this trend by offering on-site courses, seminars, and training to upgrade worker skills through immersion in standards. Proof of individual accomplishment in meeting such standards is usually acknowledged through certificates and similar official statements of completion of organized training.

The standardized certification that accreditation offers benefits many workers because it can come with increased pay and a competitive edge during downsizing or job hunting. For employers, accreditation is useful for improving productivity and service, and attracting and retaining employees. On the downside: accreditation can be a waste of time and money if it results in no useful outcome. If accreditation is mandated rather than voluntary, some employees may have no incentive to accept new information or guidance. Accreditation can be used to unfairly exclude or include applicants for jobs, and "accreditation fever" may lead some employees to a never-ending quest to acquire new certificates.

The trend toward accreditation is, of course, a gold mine of opportunity for direct marketers, telemarketers, and seminar hustlers out to take advantage of the latest fad. As the market grows, such behavior can be expected, along with the potential for conflicting standards, tests, and accreditation authorities. On the other hand, increasing interest and information will expose more job positions to the advantages of legitimate and appropriate standardization.

In many areas of employment, experience and on-the-job training have traditionally encompassed the entire set of skills necessary for a trade or profession. In positions and work areas where new community problems, social changes, or new technology have outdated such learning methods, standardized training and accreditation can replace traditional training. In some areas, however, accreditation may quickly become just another overused and exploited method of providing job perks and status without a commensurate improvement in job quality.

Areas where accreditation can be expected to grow include public-sector work, nonprofit and volunteer groups, management, consulting, and "customer-service" and "total-quality-management" oriented training. (Customer service and total quality management are both business concepts that have recently become very popular.) The greatest advantages of standardized training not now being widely implemented are in people-oriented skills such as sales positions.

At the leading edge, more regional and national training centers and accreditation bureaus will appear, organized and run on the model of colleges or existing jobs-skills facilities. Because of job requirements, however, most training will be done in blocks, with short one-day to one-week courses culminating in certificates. Employers and employees will also use on-site training, as well as distance-learning methods that offer specialized degrees and educational certificates for some courses. (See also "Distance-Learning Update," page 200.)

JOBS AND EDUCATION

On-the-Job Training in the 1990s: Customized

With vestiges that date back hundreds of years to traditional apprenticeships, medieval guilds, and other forms of hands-on experience, the recent emphasis on on-the-job training is not only an exploration of new and improved methods of improving productivity and quality, but a growing response to deficiencies of the contemporary educational system. The 1992 National Norms Study from Wonderlic Personnel Test, Inc., noted a significant negative turn in the ability level of job applicants for the first time in more than 50 years. Part of this decline is linked to a decline in "educational predictability," a factor that measures expected knowledge and reasoning ability by years of schooling. In other words, less can be expected from any given educational level today; students appear to have less ability on the average than those with the same level of education in previous generations.

Most people applying for specific jobs are potentially capable of doing the job; they intuitively understand how capable they are. In the new job market, however, this self-controlling mechanism is changing, and more applicants are applying for jobs they cannot do. Some professionals in personnel services believe this change is due to the sudden appearance of job skills—using computers and other high technology that have no traditional base in society. At the same time, shifting educational and cultural standards have made more young adults aspire to do more ambitious things with their lives. The result is higher employee turnover, increased training costs, and greater difficulty in upgrading technology.

Recognizing the problem has led to the first steps in providing solutions. Improving the educational system is an obvious direction, but one that will take years to have a noticeable effect. Instead, many companies are working on more controllable fixes with quicker response time.

Some businesses hire workers directly out of high school and enroll them in work-study programs that result in college degrees and custom-trained employees. Higher-education facilities, especially two-year community colleges, are increasingly providing "customized training" to fulfill this kind of education as well as the ongoing training upgrades necessary in the modern workplace. Faculty members—often part-time staff members—may travel to job sites to conduct classes and deliver customized course materials that link actual job experiences to the learning experience; about half of customized training courses are held on job sites. AT&T has even provided its own engineers to teach instructors what their trainees need to know.

Customized training is thought to be about ten years old in the community-college system. Varying shares of the costs may be covered by public funds. Some states, including Oregon, Colorado, North Carolina, and Texas, have been particularly assertive in providing funding. Not surprisingly, their programs have higher-than-average participation rates.

In some cases, state funds have been diverted from programs used to help relocate businesses into the state to programs subsidizing expansion and work force retraining for in-state business as part of a general economic development plan. Businesses that use such programs typically pay some portion. In Colorado, for example, state funds cover about 30 percent of the total.

Customized training differs from vocational training in that it is often provided on site and applies directly to trainees' job requirements. It is also more likely than vocational study to include subjects such as organization skills, management, and teamwork. Customized training programs also typically evolve to fit the changing requirements of the client businesses and often involve technical training, computer use, supervision, and work place literacy. Single courses are giving way to ongoing education, followup study, and continuing analysis to keep pace with the requirements of individual workplaces and provide more effective results. Customized training is also increasingly providing a more "liberal arts" approach to job skills, emphasizing flexibility, thinking skills, and teamwork rather than specialized mastery of specific tasks. Partnerships with colleges and universities for customized training can even include certificate awards and course credits applicable toward degrees. (See also "Learning to Earn," page 194.)

During the 1987-88 school year, Front Range Community College in Westminster, Colorado, had 2 customized training clients and 300 trainees. By 1991-92, the program had grown to 91 clients and 6,500 trainees. Revenue also increased, from about $100,000 to $1.4 million. This is helping boost community-college involvement, because many are seeing static or declining revenues from traditional students. The response is not universal, however. While large companies have adequate

JOBS AND EDUCATION

budgets to accommodate retraining and ongoing education, smaller companies are much less likely to be able to afford such activities.

Recent studies by The American Society for Training and Development and the League for Innovation in the Community College show that workers with formal on-the-job training have at least a 25 percent earnings advantage over those without it. Nationwide, an estimated $30 billion per year is spent on formal training and development programs in the workplace; about one in ten workers receives such training.

Employers provide about two-thirds of this training themselves. The rest is supported by colleges and universities, trade organizations, private companies, and government programs. An estimated 75 percent of U.S. community colleges are involved with customized training programs. Virtually all also provide noncustomized training courses for businesses.

Overall, however, most work-based training is informal, especially in small businesses. Informal training is three to six times more common than formal training. Traditionally, this type of one-on-one employer guidance was sufficient to pass on necessary job skills. But employers are losing their traditional capability to provide necessary job skills to employees. What smaller businesses may have once considered a luxury is increasingly becoming a necessity. With or without public funding, alliances between businesses and institutions of higher education to promote job training are certain to expand. (See also "Action-Learning Allure," page 199.)

JOBS AND EDUCATION

RESOURCES:

League for Innovation in the
Community College
Laguna Hills, CA
(714) 367-2884
(industry association of personnel
in community colleges involved in
planning and objectives)

American Society for Training and
Development
Alexandria, VA
(703) 683-8100
(industry association of professionals
in business, education, and
government working with training
and development programs)

Mel Cozzens, Department of
Business & Industry Services
Front Range Community College
Westminster, CO
(303) 466-8811 ext. 469
(community college customized-
training services)

American Association of
Community Colleges
Washington, DC
(202) 728-0200
(industry association of personnel
working with community, junior,
and technical colleges)

Wonderlic Personnel Test, Inc.
Libertyville, IL
(708) 680-4900
(standardized personnel tests)

Action-Learning Allure

One of the hottest new areas in adult education is "action learning." This concept, dating back more than 50 years, has recently become an attractive new concept in more large companies.

Action learning was created in the mid-1940s by British physicist Reginald Revans in a quest to improve training. As the name suggests, action learning involves "hands-on" experience with real-world work elements. Various versions are used in management, executive training, client services, business ethics, and sales. In practice, small groups of trainees, managers, or other employees form teams to solve real or simulated problems. The groups may attend classes or seminars, work with outside consultants, and include trained leaders or managers.

Such a program is underway at General Electric where management trainees have been sent to foreign countries to study development opportunities and assigned to sales teams working on export goals. At GE, action learning is structured into a month-long session and is required for those seeking promotions in certain areas.

The Consumer Bankers Association uses an action-learning software simulation program to train groups of bankers in real-life situations such as friendly takeovers, mergers, and acquisitions. Management teams play the roles of competing groups in preset scenarios. At Aetna Insurance, a software program known as AMP (for Aetna Management Process) is used in all phases of problem solving, including training. It has information on procedures for specific problems and applications, examples, progress checks, analytic tools, and coaching support. Other companies reported to use action-learning programs include Du Pont, Mobil Oil, Arthur Young, Consumer Bankers Association, Dun & Bradstreet, GTE, and Corning Glass.

Action learning may soon become a major focus for reform. According to several surveys, only about 20 percent of the skills that managers and executives need to perform their jobs was acquired in formal training environments such as business schools. Since the bulk of business acumen is learned on the job, the current trend toward on-the-job training is likely to prove a welcome alternative, or at least adjunct, to classroom instruction.

RESOURCES:

Wick & Company
Wilmington, DE
(302) 651-9425
(executive management consulting)

Paris/Casey, Inc.
Portland, OR
(503) 287-7000
(management consulting)

AEtna Insurance
Hartford, CT
(203) 273-0123
(insurance underwriter)

General Electric Company
Fairfield, CT
(203) 373-2211
(manufacturer of industrial and consumer products, communications, and financial services)

Consumer Bankers Association
Arlington, VA
(703) 276-1750
(industry association of federally insured deposit-taking institutions)

Distance-Learning Update

Perhaps the first modern example of distance-learning technology is the telephone, patented in 1876 by Alexander Graham Bell. Bell intended, and so stated in the patent application, that this device be used for educational lectures. Distance learning is becoming a major force in education because of the growing demand among adults for more access to learning materials and ongoing education. Beyond the telephone, technology such as fax machines, video-conferencing, satellite links, cable television, personal computers, and e-mail, make distance learning possible. But the technology alone would not create demand for distance learning. Distance learning already encompasses most of the standard educational market, from elementary school to graduate degrees. Ventures involve existing educational institutions, government organizations, and profit-making companies. The expanding market should keep distance learning on the fast track for the rest of the decade.

JOBS AND EDUCATION

Mind Extension University (ME/U) is at the forefront of the commercial operations providing education to the public. ME/U is an outgrowth of Jones Intercable, one of the largest cable-television companies in the U.S. It offers a range of courses from undergraduate subjects to advanced degree study, provided by a group of accredited colleges and universities that already offer the courses in traditional campus settings. People enrolled in the cable-televised versions (also offered as a videotape series for those without cable) are "regular" students, in that they pay their fees and have to interact with teachers to get credit for their work.

One of the most intriguing factors of the ME/U pioneering program is that less than 10 percent of viewers actually sign up for courses. Most of the more than 23 million homes that receive this programming are participating in one of the most significant trends now underway in the television industry, watching information as entertainment. The disparity between viewers and enrollees is not cause for alarm at this educational channel, however, because the program is making enough profit to expand.

Plans for ME/U call for a change in the accreditation structure. The channel itself plans to become an independent, accredited institution of higher learning, initiating and running its own courses. Viewers could then choose from a greater range of structured course plans leading to degrees and certificates in a variety of fields.

Distance-learning bottlenecks will probably proliferate around issues such as interactivity. Static viewing—or reading, for that matter—has limited educational potential. Telephones, video, and computers are all being employed in the effort to connect teachers and students, providing conversational links, conferencing, questions and answers, and personal monitoring of educational progress.

The next stage of distance-learning technology could be distance libraries. Preliminary offerings in this area include some required readings put into electronic form for online retrieval. So far, only computer connections have proven adequate, but additional transmission possibilities may appear within a few years, including cable connections. At this point, electronic text is usually stored and offered in a simple ASCII format. With the proliferation of faster, more powerful computers, however, such character-based access will be replaced by the storage and transfer of complete, high-resolution images of book text and illustrations.

Leading developers of interactive distance-learning technology include Hewlett-Packard and AT&T. Hewlett-Packard's Information

Technology Education Network uses "response terminals," computer terminals with response keypads linked to an instructor at a central terminal. Hewlett-Packard provides facilities in major cities around the world that administer text, voice, graphics, and test questions from a command-center console. Video cameras provide the instructor with visual feedback from remote classrooms. The system is used primarily for training and on-the-job education for businesses with widespread facilities. AT&T's network technology uses fiber optics, the Synchronous Optical Network (SONET). In one demonstration, an estimated 3 million students in the U.S., Canada, and Mexico got together for an interactive science and technology lesson. A smaller, full-time use of this system is the Interactive Distance Learning Project that links seven schools in a 100-square-mile region in Wisconsin. Students can now participate in studies such as foreign languages that attract too few students at a single location to permit a full-time teacher.

Ameritech Services uses the SuperSchool system to link schools in five midwestern and southern states with two-way video routed through fiber optics. Additional links allow online connections between personal computers, permitting students, teachers, and parents access to data, homework information, and communications.

Last but not least, the state of Iowa will be wired with 2,800 miles of fiber-optic cable by fall 1994. This system will transmit data, voice, and video between state agencies, libraries, and colleges. In the latter application, campuses will exchange broadcasts of classes.

RESOURCES:

Hewlett-Packard Company
Palo Alto, CA
(415) 857-1501
(computer and communications
networking services)

AT&T Learning Network
(800) 367-7225
(interactive distance-learning
systems)

Ameritech Services, Inc.
Hoffman Estates, IL
(312) 750-5000
(telecommunications services)

MFS Telecom, Inc.
Oakbrook Terraces, IL
(708) 218-7200
(manufacturer of electronic
communications equipment)

Managing Technology

One of the fastest-growing specialties in advanced education is the Management of Technology degree (MOT), a niche area of masters' business programs. The MOT trend is directly linked to a report issued in 1987 by the National Research Council that emphasized the need for interdisciplinary education in managing technology.

First offered at the Massachusetts Institute of Technology (in place before the NRC report), as of 1993, at least ten universities had instituted MOT programs, including Northwestern University, Case Western Reserve, University of Maryland, Rensselaer Polytechnic Institute, University of Denver, University of Minnesota, Georgia Tech, and the University of Miami. Northwestern and MIT also offer PhDs in the management of technology. Many of these programs are so new that the first students have yet to graduate.

Instead of a narrow focus in a specialized area, MOT programs attempt to create individuals capable of dealing with the complex, rapidly changing industry involved with technological research, development, and manufacturing. Coursework includes traditional business management studies, intellectual property concerns, risk assessment, marketing, and engineering. According to Richard Mignogna, director of the MOT program at the University of Denver, "Managing technology isn't just managing engineers and scientists. It involves capital resource allocation and human resource management—how a company decides strategically what technologies it should have and how it acquires that technology."

This interdisciplinary approach, as well as the emerging demand for such programs, gives MOT programs added clout in their institutional environments. Not yet mired in traditional educational structures and bureaucracy—an estimated 75 percent of faculty come from industry, rather than academia—MOT departments are often creative, flexible, and nontraditional in fulfilling their missions. There are no traditional models upon which to base the new studies, so programs vary in scope and content.

One indication that interest is strong: some employers who offer ongoing education funding for employees request that employees fulfill this study in MOT programs. Senior IBM executives are taking MOT programs at MIT. Students attracted to this new discipline range from recent college graduates to working professionals seeking more specialization. Schools offer both full-time and continuing-education programs to accommodate student schedules. MOT programs may even further erode the already declining popularity of the traditional MBA, providing a more attractive alternative in the changing job marketplace of the 1990s.

RESOURCES:

University of Denver Management
of Technology Program
Denver, CO
(303) 871-3155
(university graduate business
program)

American Management Association
New York, NY
(212) 586-8100
(industry association for managers in
commerce, government, nonprofit
organizations, and university
teachers of management)

National University Continuing
Education Association
Washington, DC
(202) 659-3130
(industry association of personnel
and institutions involved with
extension and continuing-
education programs)

National Society of Professional
Engineers
Alexandria, VA
(703) 684-2800
(industry association of engineers)

Supply and Demand for Professionals

Career choices for professionals through the end of the decade may be affected by factors such as population aging, shifts in cultural priorities, and current occupation levels. Especially for doctors and lawyers, the realities of the past few decades may shift significantly.

MEDICAL CAREER SHIFTS A glut of medical specialists, coupled with growing pressure to reform this segment of health care, is likely to discourage many students from following this path in advanced studies. At the same time, a nationwide dearth of primary-care doctors—especially internists, family practitioners, and pediatricians—is encouraging medical students to pursue these more traditional medical careers. Already, many medical schools are restructuring, adding more classes

SCHOOL STATISTICS

(numbers in thousands)

	1994	1984	percent change 1984-1994
K-12 enrollment	49,661	44,908	11%
Public	44,187	39,208	13
Private	5,474	5,700	-4
College enrollment (4-year)	8,984	7,711	17
Public colleges	6,085	5,198	17
Private colleges	2,899	2,513	15
Full-time students	6,070	5,395	13
Part-time students	2,914	2,317	26
College enrollment (2-year)	5,389	4,531	19
Public	5,121	4,279	20
Private	268	252	6
Full-time students	1,891	1,704	11
Part-time students	3,498	2,827	24
Degrees conferred:			
Associate	492	452	9
Bachelor's	1,166	974	20

Source: Projections of Education Statistics to 2003, *U.S. Department of Education, National Center for Education Statistics, December 1992. Projections are "middle alternative."*

JOBS AND EDUCATION

in general medicine, counseling more students to become generalists, and providing more scholarships and financial aid for those interested in these fields. According to the American Academy of Family Physicians, family-practice residency programs were 77 percent filled in 1993. A year earlier, only 67 percent of positions were filled.

Between 1965 and 1990, the number of residency cardiologists grew 734 percent, compared with just 66 percent for primary-care physicians. Although the American College of Physicians and the American Academy of Family Practice are actively lobbying to promote general practice over specialization, projections indicate a more balanced medical profession is unlikely until after the turn of the century. In the interim, more positions, if not more income opportunity, await medical students willing to make the change.

LAWYER GLUT Increasing numbers of law-school graduates and decreasing numbers of new jobs have created a pool of excess attorneys in the past few years. Reports from some law schools indicate that unemployment rates for recent graduates have risen as high as 20 percent. The results: more competition for job openings; firms becoming more selective in taking on new hires; and more recent graduates selecting work in government agencies, nonprofit associations, and other noncommercial sectors. The glut will benefit consumers. Eager young attorneys may offer services at lower rates than established firms, providing downward pressure on fees. The climate also offers potential for developing new entrepreneurial ventures, such as flat-rate legal services, specialty services, and targeting niche population or industry groups as clients.

SCIENTISTS While not yet endemic, increasing unemployment in some scientific fields indicates imbalances in some areas. Currently oversupplied areas include physicists, mathematicians, chemists, geologists, oceanographers, meteorologists, statisticians, economists, psychologists, aeronautical engineers, civil engineers, chemical engineers, electronics engineers, industrial engineers, metallurgists, nuclear engineers, and petroleum engineers.

RESOURCES:

American Bar Association
Chicago, IL
(312) 988-5000
(industry association for attorneys)

American Association for the
Advancement of Science
Washington, DC
(202) 326-6400
(industry association of scientists,
scientific societies, and professional
organizations)

American Medical Association
Chicago, IL
(312) 464-4818
(industry association of medical
professionals)

CONTRACTS UP FOR GRABS

(major collective bargaining agreements that will end or be open for renegotiation in 1994)

industry	number of agreements	number of workers covered (in thousands)
Apparel and other textile products	16	129
Chemicals and allied products	7	9
Communications	9	15
Construction	75	186
Eating and drinking establishments	1	3
Electric, gas, and sanitary services	23	54
Electronic and other electric equipment	10	96
Fabricated metal products	4	7
Finance, insurance, and real estate	6	41
Food and kindred products	16	58
Furniture and fixtures	0	0
Health services	7	10
Hotels and other lodging	4	21
Musical instruments and related products	1	4
Leather and leather products	1	2
Local government	77	213
Lumber and wood products (except furniture)	3	6
Machinery (except electrical)	7	23
Mining	1	2
Misc. manufacturing industries	2	3

industry	number of agreements	number of workers covered (in thousands)
Motor freight transportation and warehousing	7	167
Paper and allied products	8	11
Petroleum and coal products	0	0
Primary metal industries	7	38
Printing and publishing	4	7
Railroad transportation	1	2
Retail trade (except eating and drinking establishments)	42	152
Rubber and misc. plastics products	7	34
Services (except hotels and health)	6	30
State government	34	136
Stone, clay, and glass products	2	2
Textile mill products	2	7
Tobacco products	1	1
Transportation equipment	15	44
Transportation (except railroads and motor freight)	21	104
Wholesale trade	3	5
TOTAL	**430**	**1,620**

Source: Monthly Labor Review, *Bureau of Labor Statistics, January 1993*

JOBS AND EDUCATION

JOB LOSSES

(occupations with the largest projected numeric declines in employment, 1990-2005)

occupation	number of jobs lost (in thousands)	percent change 1990-2005
Farmer operators and managers	200	-16%
Bookkeeping, accounting, and auditing clerks	133	-6
Child-care workers (private)	124	-40
Sewing-machine operators, garment	116	-20
Electrical and electronic assemblers	105	-45
Typists and word processors	103	-11
Cleaners and servants (private)	101	-25
Farm workers	92	-11
Electrical and electronic equipment assemblers, precision	81	-48
Textile draw-out and winding machine operators and tenders	61	-31
Switchboard operators	57	-23
Machine-forming operators and tenders, metal and plastic	43	-25
Machine-tool-cutting operators and tenders, metal and plastic	42	-29
Telephone and cable-TV line installers and repairers	40	-30
Central-office and PBX installers and repairers	34	-43
Central-office operators	31	-59
Statistics clerks	31	-36

occupation	number of jobs lost (in thousands)	percent change 1990-2005
Packaging and filling machine operators and tenders	27	-8%
Telephone station installers and repairers	26	-55
Bank tellers	25	-5
Lathe and turning machine tool setters and set-up operators, metal and plastic	20	-24
Grinders and polishers, hand	19	-23
Electromechanical equipment assemblers, precision	18	-37
Grinding-machine setters and set-up operators, metal and plastic	18	-25
Service-station attendants	17	-7
Directory-assistance operators	16	-59
Butchers and meat cutters	14	-6
Chemical equipment controllers operators, and tenders,	14	-19
Drilling and boring machine tool setters and set-up operators, metal and plastic	13	-26
Meter readers, utilities	12	-25

Source: Outlook: 1990-2005: Occupational Employment, *Bureau of Labor Statistics, May 1992*

JOB GAINS

(occupations with the largest projected numeric increases in employment, 1990-2005)

occupation	number of jobs gained (in thousands)	percent change 1990-2005
Salespeople, retail	887	25%
Registered nurses	767	44
Cashiers	685	26
General office clerks	670	25
Truck drivers, light and heavy	617	26
General managers and top executives	598	19
Janitors, cleaners, maids, and housekeepers	555	19
Nursing aides, orderlies, and attendants	552	43
Food-counter, fountain, and related workers	550	34
Waiters and waitresses	449	26
Teachers, secondary school	437	34
Receptionists and information clerks	422	47
Systems analysts and computer scientists	366	79
Food-preparation workers	365	32
Child-care workers (nonprivate)	353	49
Gardeners and groundskeepers	348	40

occupation	number of jobs gained (in thousands)	percent change 1990-2005
Accountants and auditors	340	35%
Computer programmers	317	56
Teachers, elementary	313	23
Guards	298	34
Teacher aides and educational assistants	278	34
Licensed practical nurses	269	42
Clerical supervisors and managers	263	22
Home health aides	263	92
Cooks, restaurant	257	42
Maintenance repairers, general utility	251	22
Secretaries (except legal and medical)	248	8
Cooks, short-order and fast-food	246	33
Stock clerks, sales floor	209	17
Lawyers	206	35

JOBS AND EDUCATION

Source: Outlook: 1990-2005: Occupational Employment, *Bureau of Labor Statistics, May 1992*

FASHION

FASHION

Textured fabrics are in, and that means a boost for natural fibers like linen, silk, and wool. As the retro-1960s look becomes less popular with women, they will be downdressing in secondhand clothes. Men will sport fitted suits in lighter colors, and their ties will become narrower. Value will be the theme that continues to dominate fashion in 1994.

FASHION

Fabric Trends

One of the hottest areas in fashion for 1994 will be fabric texture. This movement is an outgrowth of recent industry and consumer interest in environmental issues, resulting in greater emphasis on natural fabrics, designs from nature, and traditional—meaning pre-high-tech—fashion elements.

The new textures emphasize natural fiber elements of linen, silk, cotton, and wool, although blends of these with man-made fibers are also being explored. Terms such as "barkweave" and "basketweave" will be evident, referring to fabric designs borrowed from the past. Newer elements include prewrinkled linens, sunbleaching, twist yarns, sandblasting, and other surface-distressing treatments.

Fabric in general will continue to be influenced by nature. The biggest winner will be flax, the parent plant of linen. Linen and linen blends will dominate many areas of the clothing industry. Genuine linen products are expected to experience strong growth, especially in the upscale and luxury market, with some help from linen blends.

Texture trends also include the expanded use of velvet materials, generally in lighter weights than in previous years. The new velvets are more likely to be machine washable and to feature solid colors with "surface interest," such as antiquing. Velvet blends will also proliferate, as cotton mixes with silk and rayon, among other fibers.

Texture is making a big splash in swimwear too. Cable-knit swimsuits, first introduced in fall 1993, are one example. Knits, crochet, textured solids, and velvet will also add more surface interest as part of this trend.

FASHION

RESOURCES:

International Linen Promotion
Commission
New York, NY
(212) 685-0424
(industry association of European
flax processors and linen weavers
promoting linen use in the U.S.)

Knitted Textile Association
New York, NY
(212) 689-3807
(industry association and
manufacturers of knitted fabrics)

Denim Trends

Denim may soon become the most distinguished American symbol worldwide, ahead of even Mickey Mouse, McDonald's, and Arnold Schwarzenegger. Because of the unrelenting popularity of denim clothes, particularly jeans, the fabric is not likely to be supplanted here at home either. The U.S. produced 750 million square feet of denim in 1991. In 1993, that figure ballooned to an estimated 1 billion square feet, a growth rate of 33 percent in only two years. Why is denim so popular these days? One major factor is a gradual change over the past decade from its primary appeal as a spring and summer seasonal fabric to a year-round fashion choice. Denim choices are broadening in other ways, with more colors and fabric weights—"light denim," for instance. Indigo Lite from Bibb is a blend of traditional denim cotton and tencel, a new rayon-based fiber from Courtaulds Fibers.

Styles are changing, too. Although the traditional western-jeans style will predominate, the newest style trend among fashion-conscious adults and teens is baggy. Baggy means bigger, and pants styles for denims—as for fashionable pants in other fabrics—will call for more material. Wide legs will be the major statement. (See "Bell Avoidance" on page 220.)

Taking a cue from colors and fabric weaves traditionally used in heavy-duty industrial-wear denims, new denim colors will include khaki, greens, and grays previously seen only on factory floors. Herringbone weaves will also mimic this blue-collar style. Other trends include stonewash variations, especially dark washes; tone-on-tone; overdyes; brushed, suede-inspired, soft looks; worn surfaces and distressed treatments (mostly sandblasting); and stripes, from thin to wide.

In an environmentally aware era, most denim makers are switching to manufacturing methods that use less toxic methods of preparing and dying fabric. Some all-natural denims are already on the market.

RESOURCES:

Levi's Naturals
Levi Strauss & Company
San Francisco, CA
(415) 544-6000
(denim clothing manufacturers)

Courtaulds Fibers, Inc.
New York, NY
(212) 944-7400
(fiber and fabric manufacturer)

Cotton, Incorporated
New York, NY
(212) 586-1070
(industry association of cotton producers)

FASHION

Women's Wear

The general trend for women's fashion, as with much of the retail environment in the United States, is toward lower prices. Even exclusive designers are entering the value fray to become more competitive in the mainstream marketplace.

BELL AVOIDANCE Bell bottoms, part of the 1960s retro trend still in vogue, have not attracted much of a mass market audience. Bell bottoms may fade as a fashion statement in 1994, but other pants of similar styles are expected to take off, including flare-bottoms, stovepipes, and sailor pants.

STYLE HIGHLIGHTS On the way in: short shorts, cutoffs, riding jackets and jodhpurs, vintage sunglasses, Edwardian "dandy" styles, oversized military-style coats, pantsuits, high-waisted pants, plaid leggings, and exotic closures such as knot buttons and ties. Hemlines: short for those under age 25; long for women in their late 20s and older.

SHEER MADNESS Transparent and translucent fabrics are maintaining popularity and will show up in more styles and varieties, including voiles, crepes, and chiffons. Varieties will include batiks, Asian patterns, florals, and retrolooks from the 1960s.

ORPHAN FASHION Following a twisting path through grunge and retro-1960s looks, the latest style from this direction is evolving into a downdressing statement, a voluntary poverty look. This orphan fashion includes recycled clothes from secondhand stores, mixed and layered pieces, and increasingly, deliberate ensemble fashions created just for this look. *Les Miserables* and *The Grapes of Wrath* have influenced the trend, and the Charlie Chaplin look is coming into play, too—wide pants and small jackets.

RETRO-ROARING "Retro" has become so successful as a statement representing styles from the 1950s, 1960s, and 1970s that it has become an established part of creating new fashion trends. Next in line: retro 1920s, borrowing styles from flappers and Busby Berkeley musicals.

TWIN SUITS Swimsuit trends include using different suits for different purposes—e.g., fuller styles for activities, minimum coverage for tanning. Double-duty swimsuits will add sophistication, so women can use them as evening wear with the addition of pants or a skirt. The flapper look from the 1920s will influence some swimwear design. Texture will be a major style choice (see "Fabric Trends" on page 217), and constructed looks will remain strong, featuring skirting, padding, underwires, and tucking.

MASS MARKET BEAUTY The nation's chain drugstores have initiated a widespread program to increase their sales of bath and beauty products. Expect to see more of these products at the local pharmacy: natural cosmetics and skin-care products, upscale perfumes, beauty products and fragrances marketed to women of color, intentional marketing to older women, and targeted marketing to the "lost generation," those aged 18 to 29.

EDIBLE ODORS Perfume history is ripe with examples of scents based on fruits and spices, natural products with which people are familiar. In this tradition, the latest trends promote sensory experiences that reinforce the love of food. Food-based scents include the established range of fruits—lemon, orange, grapefruit, peaches, tangerines, plums—and familiar cooking spices such as cinnamon, ginger, and cloves. The hottest new perfume base has a culinary following: vanilla.

HISTORICAL JEWELRY Jewelry design will continue to focus on native American, especially southwestern tribal designs, as well as African designs and influences. Homemade crafts are also more popular, with bead sales on the upswing. Replica and antique looks for jewelry are in, including authentic facsimiles and adaptations of historical pieces featuring gold, glass intaglio, and lapis lazuli. The hottest new metal is

FASHION

platinum; sales of platinum watches increased 1,000 percent between 1987 and 1992. So far, the trend has been limited to the luxury segment, with expensive watches from such upscale designers as Tourneau, Ebel, Bulgari, and Patek Phillippe. But as interest builds, manufacturers may produce more affordable ersatz "platinum" pieces for the mass market.

RESOURCES:

National Association of Chain Drugstores
Alexandria, VA
(703) 549-3001
(industry association of suppliers, manufacturers, owners and operators of chain drugstores)

Fashion Jewelry Association of America
Providence, RI
(401) 273-1515
(industry association of suppliers and manufacturers of jewelry)

Men's Wear

No hard evidence exists to verify this trend, but increasing anecdotal evidence points to a loosening of standards for business wear. More office workers, primarily in small businesses in the Midwest and on the West Coast, are coming to work in a wider range of less formal attire. For some men, this may involve only a slight relaxation from the standard dark suit, white shirt, and conservative tie to a sports jacket, colored shirt, and slacks. In some businesses, however, the traditional "package" look is being discarded altogether, abandoning jackets and ties. A few surveys have noted an increasing number of companies offering "casual dress" days, usually once a week, reminiscent of "dress-down" days that first gave baby boomers official permission to wear jeans to school in the early 1970s. Some workers have traditionally had looser dress codes—engineers and artists, for example—but if the casual look spreads into traditional bastions of rigid dress codes, such as the insurance industry or banking, we could be seeing the beginning of a major trend.

RESOURCES:

Men's Fashion Association of
America
New York, NY
(212) 683-5665
(industry association of suppliers,
textile manufacturers, clothing
companies, and retailers of men's
and boys' clothing)

FASHION

SUIT STYLES At least one major suit designer, Armani, will focus new suit styles on a more feminine silhouette. This look will feature more of an hourglass shape, with a high, fitted waist and soft, natural shoulders. Other jacket trends include narrower lapels and slightly longer lengths.

LIGHTEN UP The general trend in suit colors for 1994 is lighter. Following a fashion trend for men's suits in Europe, lighter tones will predominate over the darker shades in style for the past few years. Colors include tan, light brown, light blue, gray, cement, mushroom, ecru, sea foam, and teal.

TIE TRENDS The current wide-tie cycle, if not peaking, is at least not expanding. Maximum width for ties will remain under four inches, with a gradual movement back toward narrower widths. For the past few years, the general design of ties has emphasized thinness, with less bulky materials and lighter linings. This trend has been synchronous with the trend toward smaller knots, which are difficult to achieve with fatter ties.

RESOURCES:

Giorgio Armani
New York, NY
(212) 265-2760
(clothing wholesaler)

Burlington Menswear
Bishopville, SC
(803) 484-5436
(clothing manufacturer)

Textile Import Corporation
New York, NY
(212) 581-2840
(textile and clothing importer)

Brampton Textiles Ltd.
New York, NY
(212) 765-2510
(clothing wholesaler)

Neckwear Association of America
New York, NY
(212) 683-8454
(industry association of suppliers, fabric producers, and manufacturers of men's clothing)

FASHION

TRANSPORTATION AND TRAVEL

TRANSPORTATION AND TRAVEL

Mexico will be a favorite international vacation destination for Americans in 1994, but the days of cheap airfares may be drawing to a close. The embattled airline industry can no longer afford ultra-low fares, so the price of flying may increase 5 percent to 10 percent. Among other modes of transportation, commuter rail service is growing in popularity.

Commuting

More commuters are making a switch to train travel. Data from the public transportation industry indicate a recent increase in ridership in rail systems providing commuter transport. In 1992, the first increase since 1989 in rail commuting was reported—an additional 1.2 million passengers. Orange County and San Diego (California), the Tri-County Commuter Rail system in Florida, and the Maryland Mass Transit system led the way in boosted commuter rail traffic.

Commuting by rail includes subways (considered heavy-rail), commuter rail, and light rail. Commuter rail lines are heavy-rail systems that generally operate between municipalities, while light-rail lines use smaller lighter equipment and usually run for shorter distances than their heavy-rail cousins. The 18 light-rail systems currently in operation are attracting the most attention. Information from the American Public Transit Association indicates that at least 30 metropolitan areas are planning new systems or extensions of existing systems.

While commuter rail traffic is up, overall commuting on public transportation is not faring well. According to the 1990 census, 5.3 percent of all commutes were via public transportation, down from 6.4 percent in 1980. In most major cities, of course, reliance on public transportation is much higher than the national average. In New York City, more than 80 percent of all workers rely on public transportation. In Chicago, the share is about 75 percent; in Philadelphia, 60 percent; in Portland, 40 percent; and in Oakland, 30 percent.

In the 1980s, expenditures of public funds for mass-transit systems grew from about $2 billion to almost $4.5 billion. Much of this money has gone for new and expanded rail-based commuter systems.

Commuters generally have more positive feelings about light rail when such systems are available as alternatives to buses, subways, and vans. Housing, retail, and office construction is increasingly likely to be planned near light-rail routes. Business and residential plans in San Diego, San Francisco, Portland, and Washington, D.C., have been made with proximity to light rail in mind. Retail investment close to light-rail lines is high. The Metrorail system based in Washington, D.C., has accounted for an estimated $15 billion of nongovernment development, and the local rail system in Atlanta has reportedly brought in $70 billion in development close to the system's transfer points.

However, simply constructing more rail systems for commuters will not guarantee they will be used. The most significant factor to ensure more patronage is location. Rail service must conveniently connect residential areas—both inner-city and suburban—with centers of work. Because of the inherent flaw of suburban housing—spread out and rarely organized around centralized points—it is much more difficult to achieve high usage of light-rail links to suburban areas. Compromises include "park and ride" depots, secondary bus connections, and multimodal terminals.

Unlike bus routes, which can change overnight, rail routes become permanent fixtures in communities. Within a few years of their establishment, the flow of commuters attracts entrepreneurs offering day-care centers, fast-food outlets, dry cleaners, flower shops, convenience stores, etc. So, even though the cities with the highest commuter traffic on public transportation do not operate at a net profit, commuter-rail systems may prove profitable for cities in the long run.

Rail service for business travelers will improve even more throughout the remainder of the decade because of a blossoming relationship between privately owned railroads and local and regional public-transportation agencies. Companies such as Southern Pacific are using existing rail lines and rights of way and cutting lucrative deals for commuter-rail services to use their tracks and property. In California, such deals have expanded rail service in Los Angeles, the San Francisco Peninsula, and regions north and east of San Francisco. Other deals are under discussion or development in Denver, Portland, Sacramento, Phoenix, Salt Lake City, Dallas, Houston, and Seattle.

As the value and popularity of rail-based passenger service heats up, railways may add longer routes. Prototype mid-distance routes outside the heavily developed Northeast already being developed or expanded include links between San Francisco and southern California cities, a link between Phoenix and Tucson, a high-speed rail link between Houston, Dallas-Ft. Worth, and Austin, and a hookup between Seattle and Portland, Oregon.

Commuter-rail and light-rail transit programs currently under construction or in the planning stages include:

- **Dallas Area Rapid Transit** (DART), Dallas, Texas. 20 miles of light rail.

- **St. Louis Light Rail** (Metrolink), St. Louis, Missouri. Extension of system to 18 miles, linking East St. Louis and downtown to the airport.

- **MARTA,** Atlanta, Georgia. Northern extension for light rail.

- **Los Angeles.** Extension of the newly opened system from downtown to Long Beach.

- **New York City Transit Authority,** New York, New York. 73rd Street Tunnel connection.

- **Portland, Oregon.** Light-rail extension.

- **Baltimore, Maryland.** Light-rail extension.

- **Chicago, Illinois.** Central Circulator project.

- **Bay Area Rapid Transit** (BART), San Francisco, California. Light-rail extension.

- **New Jersey Transit,** Secaucus Transfer project and Hudson River Waterfront project.

- **Boston-Portland,** Maine commuter-rail service.

- **Maryland,** MARC commuter-rail extension.

At the other extreme, rails are increasingly considered as practical links between cities and airports as is already the case in most major European cities. Various types of railroad systems for airport transportation under discussion or development include:

- **Colorado.** Denver to the new Denver International Airport.

- **Florida.** Walt Disney World to Orlando International Airport.

- **Nevada.** Las Vegas and the convention center to the airport.

- **Pennsylvania.** Pittsburgh to the Pittsburgh International Airport.

RESOURCES:

Union Pacific Railroad Company
Omaha, NE
(402) 271-5000
(railroad operations)

Burlington Northern, Inc.
Fort Worth, TX
(817) 878-2000
(railroad operations)

TRANSPORTATION AND TRAVEL

Southern Pacific
San Francisco, CA
(415) 541-1000
(railroad operation)

Atchison, Topeka, and Santa Fe
Railway Company
Schaumburg, IL
(708) 995-6000
(railroad operations)

Federal Transit Administration
Washington, DC
(202) 366-4043
(government agency working with
mass transportation)

American Public Transit Association
Washington, DC
(202) 898-4000
(industry association of North
American public-transportation
systems, suppliers, and
manufacturers)

National Railroad Passenger
Corporation (Amtrak)
Washington, DC
(202) 484-7540
(semi-government agency operating
rail-passenger systems)

Bus Power Alternatives

Nationwide, local and regional bus companies are actively beginning to
try out available alternatives for diesel-powered vehicles from new fuel
sources to new engine technology. Alternative power sources include
methanol, LPG (liquefied petroleum gas), CNG (compressed natural gas),
electric motors, and "clean diesel." The latter modifies existing diesel
engines and fuel to improve combustion and emissions.

One such diesel fuel substitute is "biodiesel" fuel. Biodiesel fuels
come from a variety of organic renewable sources, mostly agricultural
crops such as corn or soybeans. Already in use in Europe, biodiesel fuels
are generally usable in existing diesel engines. Use of these organically
derived fuels reduces most of the polluting emissions from engine exhaust while delivering the same mileage and power as conventional diesel
fuel. Some system operators mix them with regular diesel for best performance. The most effective source for biodiesel fuels in the U.S. will
probably be soybeans, because of the size of the industry. The National
SoyDiesel Development Board already promotes SoyDiesel, a brand-
name biodiesel fuel.

The Federal Transit Administration had received 80 applications to
demonstrate alternative bus fuels by early 1993. Combined federal, state,

and local funds invested in mass-transit alternative-fuel projects total $245 million. While no single fuel or fuel system has a clear advantage at this point, some are finding regional approval. Some cities find advantages in storage and supply that make one alternative more appropriate than others, particularly with methanol and CNG.

In the long run, most industry analysts expect electric-powered buses to win out because they use centralized—and therefore more pollution-controllable—power production. However, it may be five to ten years before adequate electric-storage systems are devised for large vehicles. The first practical electric models of smaller vehicles such as passenger cars, light delivery vans, and small commuter vans are expected to be on the market in 1994 or 1995.

Buses could also get quieter. New York City and Toronto, Canada, are testing a new high-tech noise cancellation system for buses. This system uses electronic gadgetry to remove exhaust noise by emitting sound waves configured to cancel out the sound waves produced by exhaust. In practice, the electronic mufflers reportedly eliminate up to 90 percent of the noise produced by an idling bus. Similar systems protect drivers in noise-intensive vehicles such as heavy trucks and light airplanes.

RESOURCES:

National SoyDiesel
Development Board
Jefferson City, MO
(800) 841-5849
(national organization promoting biodiesel fuels)

American Public Transit Association
Washington, DC
(202) 898-4000
(industry association of North American public-transportation systems, suppliers and manufacturers)

Noise Cancellation
Technologies, Inc.
Stamford, CT
(203) 961-0500
(sound-reduction technology)

American Bus Association
Washington, DC
(202) 842-1645
(industry association of suppliers, manufacturers, and operators of passenger buses)

Better Roads and
Transportation Council
Washington, DC
(202) 488-2722
(industry association of executives from state transportation-improvement organizations)

Airline
Hubbub

The U.S. domestic-airline industry currently bases its operations on a "hub-and-spoke" system. A series of hub airports serve as transfer and destination points, and major airlines schedule most flights to take advantage of the greatest number of passengers passing through these centers. Travelers located in nonhub cities must generally rely on indirect flights to get to most destinations, with multiple flights routed through hub centers.

Despite its disadvantages, this system makes it easier for airlines to keep a maximum number of passengers on most flights. But continued losses and shakeups in the industry increase the likelihood that the hub system may evolve into something else. Some airports used as smaller hubs have already been eliminated by a few airlines, including Washington's National Airport, and airports in Dayton and Milwaukee. Other cities facing cutbacks in service and potential loss of hub status include Cleveland, Nashville, Raleigh-Durham, Phoenix, St. Louis, and San Jose.

The major airlines may keep their most profitable routes between the largest cities and sell off routes servicing secondary markets or develop auxiliary flight operations to service them. Flights from outlying areas may still use the biggest hubs as major destinations and transfer points using smaller planes and different schedules. The difference to passengers: longer waits, more airline switching, and higher prices.

Because of the growing number of underserved travelers living outside normal hub systems, a secondary hub system could develop. Multiple airlines could coordinate overlapping service between regions of the country with airlines, commuter flights, and available connections to major hubs. A proliferation of choices in smaller passenger planes—including more prop-driven aircraft—increasing fuel efficiencies, lower operating costs using nonunion staffs, and improved electronic scheduling systems could make the secondary flight market a profitable enterprise. Such specialized route carriers have begun to appear in the past few years, offering competitive rates, sometimes even lower than those of major carriers. These include American Trans Air, Skybus, Reno Air, and Morris Air.

At the same time, aggressive newcomers such as Southwest Airlines are assaulting the major airlines. Southwest was already in place on several main West Coast air routes with discount fares and began a move into East Coast territory in mid-1993. Unlike past fare wars between the largest competitors, airlines such as Southwest are set up—through lean management structure, low overhead, nonunion labor, and minimal service on most flights—to operate with permanent low fares. Southwest Airlines also picks relatively short routes and routinely chooses airports outside the congested hub system. In 1993, United Airlines, possibly influenced by Southwest's operating style, reportedly began discussing its own nonunion, low-overhead spinoff airline to service secondary, short-haul routes.

Lower rates are likely to be an exception in the near future, however. Established airlines cannot offer low rates and maintain profits. Cheap air travel is likely to be confined to nonhub cities and routes serviced by startup companies. Most travelers can expect average fare increases of 5 to 10 percent in 1994. Within a few years, the mix of major routes and hubs serviced by large established airlines and secondary routes serviced by startup airlines could reverse pricing structure to high prices for most frequented routes and low prices elsewhere. Although some people only fly when the price is right, most business fliers depend on air travel to get to most locations and are unlikely to abandon the skies if prices rise.

RESOURCES:

Air Transportation Association
of America
Washington, DC
(202) 626-4000
(industry association of airline
companies)

American Trans Air, Inc.
Indianapolis, IN
(317) 247-4000
(passenger airline)

Reno Air, Inc.
Reno, NV
(702) 829-5100
(passenger airline)

Morris Air Service, Inc.
Salt Lake City, UT
(801) 466-7747
(passenger airline)

TRANSPORTATION
AND TRAVEL

Mexican Vacations

Travel to Mexico may become more familiar to Americans in the near future. Taking advantage of increasing prosperity in that country, the already high volume of Americans heading south, and the impending reduction of business restrictions created by the North American Free Trade Agreement, more U.S. companies, from retail outlets to hotels, are establishing bases and expanding operations in Mexico. Other factors influencing growth in the Mexican travel market include more roads connecting smaller cities and towns, expanding franchised service stations, improvements in local and regional telephone service, and more support from Mexican tourist authorities.

Outside established tourist bases and Mexico City, U.S. lodging companies have much room to expand. One of the biggest potential profit makers will be motels and limited-service facilities, now a significant part of the U.S. lodging industry. These lower-cost units offer greater opportunity for travel on a limited budget, especially for leisure travelers and families. As the general business scene also expands, there should be a much larger market for business travelers seeking lower-priced accommodations, too.

Mexico will also improve its air links, both within the country and with major U.S. cities. Along with these expanded connections, car rentals should proliferate. Guide services, organized tours, adventure trips, outdoor experiences, and other aspects of contemporary vacationing will also improve and increase in availability. A delay or negative outcome in Congress for NAFTA should have little effect on increasing American tourism in Mexico, since the relative affordability of travel in that country continues to attract value-conscious vacationers. When and if it does take effect, NAFTA will first make its presence known in

TRANSPORTATION AND TRAVEL

already urbanized areas and along the border. One visible effect may be the "Americanization" of the Mexican retail industries, from fast food to shopping outlets.

Major U.S. shopping-mall developers are already hard at work south of the border, creating new urban shopping environments modeled after the American system. With a newly emerging middle class, a rising standard of living for most Mexican citizens, and increasing numbers of foreign visitors, this U.S. retail invasion is unlikely to abate soon, and will include expansions for Wal-mart, Kmart, McDonald's, Pizza Hut, 7-Eleven, Radio Shack, and many others.

Because most of the Americanized retail presence will be in close proximity to major cities and established resort areas, a secondary travel market is likely to develop for gringos hunting for the more authentic Mexico. Many will be drawn to back-country travel, especially camping, hiking, bicycling tours, motorcycle tours, and camper treks. Private and government efforts may even develop to preserve this part of the Mexican culture for visitors and Mexican citizens, just as museums and historic preservation efforts have created major tourist destinations in the U.S.

This future may be closer than we think. Metropolitan authorities in Tijuana and Juarez have already begun constructing Mexican-history theme parks. One features a roller coaster designed in the form of Quetzalcoati, serpent god of the Aztecs, and a full-sized replica of the Aztec Pyramid of the Sun. Meanwhile, unexpected beneficiaries of the newly sanitized Mexican travel industry may be countries even further south of the border. Central-American countries, at least those with stable political conditions and safe travel, may become more appealing to adventuresome American travelers.

RESOURCE:

Mexican Government Tourism
Office
New York, NY
(212) 838-2949
(Mexican government agency
promoting travel to Mexico)

Other Travel Trends

FARM TOURS Middle-class urban interest in Midwestern farming "roots" and rising attention to ecologically based travel destinations are boosting the farm-tour business. This type of family vacation includes interactions with farm animals, rides on tractors, agricultural demonstrations, exhibits of antique equipment, and hay rides. Farm tours may also include bed-and-breakfast accommodations and special events such as county fairs and traditional local celebrations.

SPEED CHECK Improved service features at more hotels will include faster check-ins and check-outs, especially for business travelers. Technology is the answer for some of this improvement. Hotel-bill review in guests' rooms via TV is already established in many major hotels. Electronic kiosks in lobbies will provide an additional step soon, with automated self-service bill review, payment, and receipts. Remote devices can also speed up service. Travelers to the Airport Hilton in Chicago and the Opryland Hotel in Nashville can check in at the airport.

ELDER TRAVEL EXTRAS The burgeoning population of Americans aged 60 and older is a prime age group for leisure travel. Many older travelers have physical problems such as hearing loss, failing eyesight, and arthritis. In response, hotels are redesigning rooms to accommodate these and other physical handicaps. Features include large-print newspapers, telephones with volume controls, levers instead of handles on doors, handrails on tubs, wider doors for walkers and wheelchairs, and larger switches and buttons for radios and televisions. Hotels may also alter their marketing strategies to entice seniors into traveling by meeting their special needs.

SATURATED B&Bs Bed-and-breakfast inns have formed one of the fastest-growing segments of the lodging industry over the past decade. The U.S. now has more than 20,000 such establishments, up from fewer than 1,000 only ten years ago. Growth continues in some midwestern and southern states, but oversaturation is the rule in most other areas. This should mean helpful price breaks for travelers over the next few years. Competing establishments may also offer incentives such as local tour services, special events, exercise facilities, and family activities.

GREEN ROOMS Some hotels are going even further than the now-standard nonsmoking room by offering selected rooms with extra levels of air and water filtering. Such environments obviously appeal to travelers with allergies, but nonallergic lodgers are also queuing up because of real or perceived difficulties with odors from cleaning solutions, mildew, and other problems. Hotels with additional environmental filters usually charge extra for the service.

FARE INCREASES A short era of lower airline fares is gradually coming to a close, but the industry will still use "bargain" fares as a marketing strategy. While periodic fare wars may keep low-cost flights in the public mind, the trend is for the lowest fares to creep upward. In 1993, for instance, major U.S. airlines increased their lowest rates $10 to $20 and will probably do so again in 1994. At the same time, they will offer fewer fare promotions, and when they do, fewer low-cost per flight seats will be available. The estimated average fare increases for business flyers in 1994 will be 5 percent.

ELECTRONIC NAVIGATORS Beginning in 1993, the Federal Aviation Administration began testing satellite-based electronic navigation systems on commercial aircraft. The first tests, carried out by Continental Airlines using the Global Positioning System (GPS), allow more precise navigation during poor flight conditions. The GPS can improve on-time performance, reduce fuel usage, and reduce work for flight crews.

TRAVEL AGENTS In the past ten years, the number of travel agencies in the United States has doubled from 15,000 to more than 32,000. Their share of total ticket sales has also doubled from about 40 percent to 85 percent. The domination of travel agencies is not likely to end soon; the continuing complexity of routes and fares only encourages more travelers to rely on expert help in arranging their schedules. Along the same lines, more travel agencies will market their capabilities for hotel reservations, partly because the options are more confusing, but mostly because they now get commissions for referring lodgers. Some agencies may offer customized automation services to frequent flyers who know exactly what they need, cutting the agency's overhead.

RESOURCES:

American Hotel and
Motel Association
Washington, DC
(202) 289-3100
(industry association of personnel,
businesses, and organizations in the
lodging trade)

American Association of
Retired Persons
Washington, DC
(202) 434-2277
(national organization of individuals
aged 50 and older)

American Bed and
Breakfast Association
Richmond, VA
(804) 379-2222
(industry association of owners
and operators of bed-and-breakfast
establishments)

Travel Industry Association
of America
Washington, DC
(202) 293-1433
(industry association of personnel
in travel companies, chambers of
commerce, and government
departments involved in travel)

American Society of Travel Agents
Alexandria, VA
(703) 739-2782
(industry association of travel
agents, travel and touring agencies,
and travel-related businesses)

Choice Hotels International
Silver Spring, MD
(301) 593-5600
(elderly accessible lodging facilities)

O'Hare Hilton Hotel
Chicago, IL
(312) 686-8000
(off-site registration)

Opryland Hotel
Nashville, TN
(615) 889-1000
(off-site registration)

Continental Airlines, Inc.
Houston, TX
(713) 821-2100
(off-site registration)

Best Western Dubuque Inn
Dubuque, IA
(319) 556-7760
(farm tours)

Runzheimer International
Rochester, WI
(414) 767-2200
(market research)

Federal Aviation Administration
Washington, DC
(202) 267-3484
(government agency involved with
airline transportation)

TRANSPORTATION
AND TRAVEL

NINE

SPORTS AND EXERCISE

SPORTS AND EXERCISE

Walking is becoming the exercise of choice for the aging baby-boom generation, but overall, exercise is practiced by only a minority of adults. Golf, ever-popular with even sedentary Americans, is bumping up against environmental concerns in some communities because of the high level of chemical pesticides and fertilizers used to maintain lush, green links.

Exercise Trends

Successive waves of interest in various exercises have swept America in the past few decades. The country has endured periods of frenzy for jogging, tennis, racquetball, aerobics, climbing, bicycling, and weight lifting. Public interest, however, has not yet translated into mass participation for any of the above, or in fact, any form of regular exercise.

In the past few years, it has become increasingly clear that only a minority of adults are doing all of the participating. Depending on the source, between 17 and 30 percent of the population exercises regularly (at least three times a week). Ongoing surveys also indicate the share of frequent exercisers is either remaining constant or declining slightly.

Historically, people exercise less as they grow older. Since the massive baby boom is hitting middle age, this minority exercise position in the United States seems likely to grow even smaller in the future.

Currently, trends in adult exercise favor machines and devices, with stair-climbers, step equipment, and treadmills leading the pack. Stair-climbing equipment sales increased 44 percent in 1991, and treadmill sales increased 19 percent. Weight lifting is down, the latest victim of too much trendiness. In general, recent trends have begun to emphasize flexibility over strength and stamina over power. Aerobics, a former victim of oversaturation, is gaining new followers as part of this new emphasis, altered to accommodate the newer low-impact desires of the workout audience.

Beyond the hard-core center of the exercise community, a larger audience of uncommitted adults is becoming more susceptible to the exercise message: more energy and longer life through physical improvement. Surveys have shown that after age 30, adults are less likely to develop long-term exercise habits. But as they pass 40, the approach of menopause, sagging bodies, heart disease, and declining mental performance form a significant specter of mortality, making many aging boomers likely candidates for lifestyle changes.

It won't happen fast, though. Not counting the minority of change-minded people who naturally gravitate to new situations, most consumers, no matter what the danger, will not radically alter their diet or physical activities overnight. Trends in cigarette smoking, cholesterol intake, seatbelt use, and other activities show that gradual changes over long periods of time are all that can be expected.

Changes in social acceptability, evolving fashion standards, and the lure of nonthreatening activities such as golf and swimming are more likely than the threat of disease to modify the physical condition of the general population. Some exercise-industry professionals are also noting a recent change in the attitude of those involved in regular programs. The new goal is more likely to be "inner health" than exterior appearance. This attitude, linked with an aging population, will increasingly shift exercisers away from power-driven activities to those that promise improved physical well-being and increased longevity.

So far, the big winner in this trend has been walking. Recent studies point to the longevity benefits of cumulative physical activity such as walking, and walking is also a nonstressful activity. Walking surpassed swimming to become the number-one fitness activity in 1990, according to the National Sporting Goods Association, boosted in the past decade by "mall walking" programs across the country; 1994 marks the tenth anniversary of this particular phenomenon. According to Gary Yanker, author of several books about walking, mall walking was first reported in 1984 in Kansas City, Missouri.

Current trends in walking include walking routines, walking in place, backwards walking, and corporate walking programs for employees. Participation in organized walking clubs is also increasing, following the lead of traditional German and Dutch walking societies, "Volksmarching." The U.S. now has an estimated 1,000 such clubs. Walking is also becoming more attractive as a beneficial way to help recover from athletic injuries and operations, and to alleviate some chronic physical conditions such as arthritis and back pain.

For those who crave more energetic activity, some walking programs are adding features such as weights and poles. These may broaden the market for sporting-goods manufacturers in this otherwise equipment-shy trend. All athletic-shoe manufacturers have added walking models to their lines.

RESOURCES:

Walking World
New York, NY
(212) 879-5794
(consulting for exercise programs
involving walking)

Strongput, Inc.
Baltimore, MD
(410) 356-0900
(manufacturer of weight products
for walking and aerobics)

NordicTrack, Inc.
Chaska, MN
(612) 448-6987
(home-exercise equipment)

Walking Medicine
by Gary Yanker and Kathy Burton
McGraw-Hill, 1990
New York, NY
(212) 512-2000
$14.95, 480 pages

Green Golfing

The image of golf seems inextricably linked with the outdoors and nature. However, golfing is more likely to cause ecological problems than improve the planet. And with a boom in golf underway, more new golf courses and increasing environmental problems are at hand. This trend has already resulted in considerable opposition to course development. A recent survey by the American Society of Golf Course Architects reported that 39 in 40 development companies ran into difficulties over permits because of environmental concerns.

The problem is that fertilizers, pesticides, and herbicides used in abundance to maintain greens add toxic runoff in many urban areas. Some also protest the loss of natural habitat when new golf courses are built. Furthermore, golf courses use a lot of water to keep greens green, and frequent watering also facilitates the runoff of chemicals.

In response to this concern, the golf industry has been gradually reforming its methods, from more careful environmental studies before building new courses to adopting more ecologically sensitive maintenance operations. In the future, new courses will include design considerations that preserve and incorporate existing natural features such as wooded areas, wetlands, and land contours. They will take advantage of new types of grasses that require less water and are more weed- and insect-resistant. Maintenance plans will minimize use of chemicals that that can become toxic. Courses can also better control runoff with artificial ponds and areas that trap the runoff before it reaches local water systems. Golf courses are also taking lessons from the organic-gardening industry, using natural predators and improvements in site maintenance to naturally control pests.

RESOURCES:

National Golf Foundation
Jupiter, FL
(407) 744-6006
(industry association of suppliers and manufacturers of golf equipment, golf-club operators, architects and course developers, and golf instructors)

U.S. Golf Association
Far Hills, NJ
(908) 234-2300
(industry association of owners and operators of golf courses)

Other Exercise Trends

HARD HATS Bicycle riders are in the midst of a safety-minded trend; sales of bicycle helmets are way up. The public image of these safety devices seems to have improved. Fewer cyclists now resist purchasing and wearing them. Aggressive marketing campaigns and competitive pricing have also helped, along with the rapidly growing market for kids, paving the way for adult use. Safety often begins with kids. When baby boomers had children, public awareness of child safety seats boomed, too, followed by increased seat-belt use among adults.

RESOURCES

Bicycle Institute of America
Washington, DC
(202) 463-6622
(industry association of suppliers, manufacturers, and retailers of bicycles)

KID FITNESS Fueled by the increasing numbers of children born to baby boomers, the exercise industry is finding new and younger customers for classes, equipment, and training. YMCA and other facilities are reporting increases in children's attendance at exercise programs. Little Gym International is one of the first franchised exercise centers for children. It operated 34 facilities in early 1993, with planned expansion to 100 by 1994. Kidsports has 23 facilities, with 15 more planned by 1994. Forty percent of all health clubs offered programs for children in 1993. Expect more emphasis on licensing such facilities and using professional trainers experienced in child development.

RESOURCES

Association of Quality Clubs
Boston, MA
(617) 951-0055
(industry association and manufacturers of racquet-sports equipment and owners and operators of sports and exercise clubs)

Little Gym International
Kirkwood, WA
(206) 889-4588
(franchised exercise facilities for children)

Kidsports
Sinking Spring, PA
(215) 678-1630
(franchised exercise facilities for children)

PE REFORM After decades of neglect, physical fitness is again getting attention in the nation's school systems. A new generation of baby-boom parents has helped focus attention on the need for organized physical activity beyond sports teams. New directions now include less emphasis on competitive sports and more on active movement, developing coordination skills, building physical self-confidence, and establishing healthy exercise habits. At this stage, reform is mostly taking place at the elementary-school level, where the effects of proper guidance seem more effective.

RESOURCES

National Association for Sport and Physical Education
Reston, VA
(703) 476-3410
(industry association of professionals involved in sports and physical education)

American Sports Education Institute
North Palm Beach, FL
(407) 842-3600
(national organization promoting amateur sports and physical education)

CLIMB ZONES Overuse of state and national park land by rock climbers will probably result in new regulations covering climbing activities in many areas of the country. Marked climbing zones will be established, modeled after the trail system used for mountain bikes.

RESOURCES:

American Sport Climbers
Federation
New York, NY
(212) 865-4383
(national organization involved
with climbing sports)

The Access Fund
Boulder, CO
(303) 545-6772
(national organization working to
develop and protect climbing areas)

YOGA NICHES Far from being left behind by the latest modern workouts, yoga is quickly becoming one of the trendiest new exercise formats. Yoga classes are attracting exercisers burned out on high impact, strenuous workout activities. One new form is an aerobicized yoga that emphasizes cardiovascular fitness without the high energy level of regular aerobics. Yoga aficionados are also searching out types of yoga different from the hatha-yoga prototype most often taught in the U.S. such as Ashtanga, Iyengar, Jivamukti, Pranayama, Laya, Jnana, Dhyana, and Kundalini.

RESOURCES:

Yoga Journal
published by California Yoga
Teachers Association
Berkeley, CA
(510) 841-9200

Crunch Fitness

New York, NY
(212) 875-1902
(exercise club featuring "Urban
Yoga")

APPENDICES

ADDITIONAL RESOURCES

The American Forecaster Almanac is compiled from hundreds of different sources, including print publications, electronic media, and personal interviews with industry experts. Many of these sources are widely available and can provide additional information for those who are pursuing topics of interest.

Many people think of information resources as places to find answers to questions. While this is an obvious and practical use, it overlooks a critical and often undervalued method for discovery of new information: browsing. Many of the sources listed below can be invaluable tools for anyone on a quest for the unknown. Taking time to browse through these or other publications can yield results beyond the expected.

The best place to begin any search for information is a public library. School libraries can also be fruitful sources, especially those at colleges and universities. Questions? When in doubt, ask a librarian.

More information about the periodicals and books listed can be found in *Books in Print*, an annual listing of books published by R.R. Bowker; *Directory of Publications*, an annual listing of periodicals published by Gale Research; and *Ulrich's International Periodicals Directory*, an annual listing of international periodicals published by R.R. Bowker.

The listings below begin with general resources, then are organized to correspond to the chapters in this book. Information about content, subscriptions, and availability can be obtained from the telephone numbers listed with each entry. Because subscription rates can change frequently, it is always best to call to confirm the current rate, as well as other subscription qualifications. Most periodicals with controlled circulation, for instance, require subscribers to fit their industry rules before qualifying for free subscriptions.

GENERAL RESOURCES

CQ Researcher (weekly)
Congressional Quarterly, Inc.
Washington, DC
Rates upon request
Editorial: (202) 887-8500
Subscriptions: (800) 432-2250

Encyclopedia of Associations (annual)
Gale Research, Inc.
Detroit, MI
(313) 961-2242.

Encyclopedia of Information Systems and Services (irregular)
Gale Research, Inc.
Detroit, MI
(313) 961-2242

Future Vision: The 189 Most Important Trends of the 1990s
By the editors of *Research Alert*, 1991.
Sourcebooks, Inc.
Naperville, IL
(708) 961-2161

Gale Directory of Online Databases (quarterly)
Gale Research, Inc.
Detroit, MI
(313) 961-2242

Information, U.S.A.
By Matthew Lesko, 1989.
Viking Press, Penguin USA
New York, NY
(212) 366-2000

Instant Information
By Joel Makower and Alan Green
Prentice Hall, 1987.
New York, NY
(212) 373-8417

The New York Times (daily)
New York Times Company
New York, NY
Editorial: (212) 556-1234
Subscriptions: (800) 631-2500

The 1994 Information Please Business Almanac and Desk Reference
By Seth Godin, editor
Houghton Mifflin Company, 1993.
Boston, MA
(617) 351-5000

Statistical Abstract of the United States (annual)
Data Users Service Division
Bureau of the Census
Washington, DC
Editorial: (301) 763-5299
Subscriptions: Superintendent of Documents (202) 783-3238

USA Today (daily)
Gannett Company, Inc.
Arlington, VA
Editorial: (703) 276- 3400
Subscriptions: (800) 872-0001

The Wall Street Journal (daily)
Dow Jones and Company, Inc.
New York, NY
Editorial: (212) 416-2000
Subscriptions: (800) 841-8000

The World Almanac and Book of Facts (annual)
Funk & Wagnalls
Rahwah, NJ
(201) 529-6900

OVERVIEW

American Demographics (monthly)
American Demographics, Inc.
Ithaca, NY
$69
Editorial: (607) 273-6343
Subscriptions: (800) 828-1133

Current Population Reports (irregular)
Bureau of the Census
Washington, DC
$65
Editorial: (301) 763-4040
Subscriptions: Superintendent of
Documents (202) 783-3238

The Futurist (bimonthly)
World Future Society
Bethesda, MD
$30 (with membership)
Editorial/subscriptions:
(301) 656-8274

The Gallup Poll Monthly (monthly)
The Gallup Poll
Princeton, NJ
$95
($65 for nonprofit institutions)
Editorial/subscriptions:
(609) 924-9600

BUSINESS AND THE ECONOMY

Across the Board (monthly)
The Conference Board
New York, NY
$40
Editorial/subscriptions:
(212) 759-0900

American City and County (monthly)
Communication Channels, Inc.
Atlanta, GA
$56
Editorial: (404) 955-2500
Subscriptions: (708) 647-7124

American Libraries (monthly)
American Library Association
Chicago, IL
$60 (subscription with membership)
Editorial: (312) 280-4216
Subscriptions: (800) 545-2433

The Economist (weekly)
Economist Publications Ltd.
New York, NY, and London, UK
$110 (US)
Editorial: (212) 541-5730
Subscriptions: (800) 456-6086

Farm Journal (14/year)
Farm Journal, Inc.
Philadelphia, PA
$14 (controlled circulation)
Editorial/subscriptions:
(215) 829-4710

Feedstuffs (weekly)
Miller Publishing Company
Minnetonka, MN
$75
Editorial: (612) 931-0211
Subscriptions: (800) 888-7580

Forbes magazine (biweekly)
Forbes, Inc.
New York, NY
$52
Editorial: (212) 620-2200
Subscriptions: (800) 888-9896

Fortune (biweekly)
Time Warner, Inc.
New York, NY
$50
Editorial: (212) 586-1212
Subscriptions: (800) 621-8000

Industry Week (biweekly)
Penton Publishing Company
Cleveland, OH
$60 (controlled circulation)
Editorial/subscriptions:
(216) 696-7000

Kiplinger Washington Letter (weekly)
The Kiplinger Washington Editors
Washington, DC
$63
Editorial: (202) 887-6400
Subscriptions: (800) 544-0155

Library Hi Tech News (10/year)
Pierian Press
Ann Arbor, MI
$70 (individuals)
$95 (institutions)
Editorial/subscriptions:
(313) 434-5530

Library Journal (21/year)
Cahners Publishing Company
New York, NY
$71
Editorial: (212) 645-0067
Subscriptions: (800) 677-6694

Louis Rukeyser's Business Almanac
Louis Rukeyser, editor, 1991.
Simon and Schuster
New York, NY
(212) 698-7000

The Office (monthly)
Office Publications, Inc.
Stamford, CT
$40
Editorial/subscriptions:
(203) 327-9670

Predicasts Forecasts (quarterly)
Ziff Communications Company
Cleveland, OH
$850
Editorial/subscriptions:
(800) 321-6388

Survey of Current Business (monthly)
Department of Commerce
Washington, DC
$23
Editorial: (202) 606-9900
Subscriptions: Superintendent of
Documents (202) 783-3238

Urban Land (monthly)
Urban Land Institute
Washington, DC
$60 (with membership)
Editorial/subscriptions:
(202) 624-7000

U.S. Industrial Outlook (annual)
Department of Commerce
Washington, DC
$8.50
Editorial: (202) 606-9900
Subscriptions: Superintendent of
Documents (202) 783-3238

HEALTH

American Druggist (monthly)
The Hearst Corporation
New York, NY
$44
Editorial/subscriptions:
(212) 297-9680

FDA Consumer (monthly)
Office of Public Affairs
Food and Drug Administration
Rockville, MD
$12
Editorial: (301) 443-3220
Subscriptions: Superintendent of
Documents (202)783-3238

Health (bimonthly)
Hippocrates Partners
San Francisco, CA
$15.97
Editorial: (415) 512-9100
Subscriptions: (800) 274-2522

Health United States (annual)
National Center for Health
Statistics
Hyattsville, MD
$8.50 (also available on floppy disc)
Editorial: (301) 436-8500
Subscriptions: Superintendent of
Documents (202) 783-3238

Hospitals (biweekly)
American Hospital Publishing
Chicago, IL
$65
Editorial/subscriptions:
(312) 440-6800

Longevity (monthly)
Longevity International Ltd.
New York, NY
$24
Editorial: (212) 496-6100
Subscriptions: (800) 333-2782

Source Book of Health Insurance Data
(annual)
Health Insurance Association of
America
Washington, DC
Free
Editorial/subscriptions:
(202) 223-7845

SCIENCE AND COMPUTERS

Boardwatch (monthly)
Boardwatch Magazine
Littleton, CO
$36
Editorial: (303) 973-6038
Subscriptions: (800) 933-6038

Communications Week (weekly)
CMP Publications, Inc.
Manhasset, NY
$143 (controlled circulation)
Editorial: (516) 562-5530
Subscriptions: (516) 562-5882

Computer World (weekly)
CW Publishing
Framingham, MA
$42.95
Editorial: (508) 879-0700
Subscriptions: (800) 669-1002

Discover (monthly)
Walt Disney Magazine Publishing
Group, Inc.
Burbank, CA
$29.95
Editorial: (818) 567-5739
Subscriptions: (800) 829-9132

Information Week (weekly)
CMP Publications, Inc.
Manhasset, NY
$120 (controlled circulation)
Editorial: (516) 562-5695
Subscriptions: (516) 562-5882

Popular Science (monthly)
Times Mirror Magazines, Inc.
New York, NY
$13.94
Editorial: (212) 779-5000
Subscriptions: (800) 289-9399

*Predicasts Overview of Markets and
Technology (PROMPT)* (monthly)
Ziff Communications Company
Cleveland, OH
$1,000 (also available on disc)
Editorial/subscriptions:
(800) 321-6388

Science News (weekly)
Science Service, Inc.
Washington, DC
$39.50
Editorial: (202) 785-2255
Subscriptions: (800) 247-2160

The Scientist (biweekly)
The Scientist, Inc.
Philadelphia, PA
$79
Editorial/subscriptions:
(215) 386-0100

Technology Review (8/year)
Association of Alumni and Alumnae
of MIT
Cambridge, MA
$24
Editorial: (617) 253-8250
Subscriptions: (800) 877-5230

THE CONSUMER

Advertising Age (weekly)
Crain Communications, Inc.
Chicago, IL
$86
Editorial: (212) 210-0100
Subscriptions: (800) 678-9595

Adweek's Marketing Week (weekly)
Adweek L.P.
New York, NY
$75
Editorial: (212) 536-5336
Subscriptions: (800) 722-6658

Automotive News (weekly)
Crain Communications, Inc.
Detroit, MI
$75
Editorial: (313) 446-6000
Subscriptions: (800) 678-9595

Beverage Industry (monthly)
Stagnito Publishing Company
Northbrook, IL
$40 (controlled circulation)
Editorial: (708) 205-5660
Subscriptions: (708) 543-8713

Chain Store Age Executive (monthly)
Lebhar-Friedman, Inc.
New York, NY
$79 (controlled circulation)
Editorial: (212) 756-5252
Subscriptions: (813) 664-6707

Food Technology (monthly)
Institute of Food Technologists
Chicago, IL
$82
Editorial/subscriptions:
(312) 782-8424

Hardware Age (monthly)
Chilton Company
Radnor, PA
$16 (controlled circulation)
Editorial: (215) 964-4275
Subscriptions: (215) 964-4144

Interior Design (14/year)
Cahners Publishing Company
New York, NY
$39.95
Editorial: (212) 645-0067
Subscriptions: (800) 542-8138

Nation's Restaurant News (weekly)
Lebhar-Friedman, Inc.
New York, NY
$34.50
Editorial: (212) 756-5000
Subscriptions: (800) 447-7133

Progressive Grocer (monthly)
Maclean Hunter Media
Stamford, CT
$67
Editorial/subscriptions:
(203) 325-3500

ENTERTAINMENT AND
THE MEDIA

Amusement Business (weekly)
BPI Communications
Nashville, TN
$99
Editorial: (615) 321-4250
Subscriptions: (800) 999-3322

Billboard (weekly)
BPI Communications
New York, NY
$225
Editorial: (212) 764-7300
Subscriptions: (800) 669-1002

Bloomsbury Review (bimonthly)
Owaissa Communications
Denver, CO
$16
Editorial/subscriptions:
(303) 892-0620

Cablevision (biweekly)
Capital Cities Media, Inc.
New York, NY
$55
Editorial: (212) 887-8400
Subscriptions: (609) 786-0501

Editor and Publisher (weekly)
Editor and Publisher Company
New York, NY
$50
Editorial/subscriptions:
(212) 675-4380

Electronic Media (weekly)
Crain Communications, Inc.
Chicago, IL
$69
Editorial: (312) 649-5200
Subscriptions: (800) 678-9595

Publisher's Weekly (weekly)
Cahners Publishing Company
New York, NY
$129
Editorial: (212) 463-6758
Subscriptions: (800) 278-2991

Rolling Stone (biweekly)
Straight Arrow Publishers, Inc.
New York, NY
$25.95
Editorial: (212) 484-1616
Subscriptions: (800) 568-7655

Spin (monthly)
Camouflage Associates, Inc.
New York, NY
$14.95
Editorial: (212) 633-8200
Subscriptions: (800) 829-9093

Television Topics Catalog (quarterly)
Journal Graphics
Denver, CO
(call for index price)
Editorial/subscriptions:
(303) 831-9000

Variety (weekly)
Cahners Publishing Company
New York, NY
$149
Editorial: (212) 779-1100
Subscriptions: (800) 323-4345

JOBS AND EDUCATION

Inc. (monthly)
NC Publishing Company
Boston, MA
$19
Editorial: (617) 248-8000
Subscriptions: (800) 234-0999

Monthly Labor Review (monthly)
Bureau of Labor Statistics
U.S. Department of Labor
Washington, DC
$24
Editorial: (202) 606-5864
Subscriptions: Superintendent of
Documents (202) 783-3238

Occupational Outlook Quarterly
(quarterly)
Bureau of Labor Statistics
U.S. Department of Labor
Washington, DC
$6.50
Editorial: (202) 606-5864
Subscriptions: Superintendent of
Documents (202) 783-3238

Projections of Education Statistics to 2001, An Update, 1990
National Center for Education Statistics
U.S. Department of Education
(202) 219-1651

FASHION

America's Textile International (monthly)
Billian Publishing, Inc.
Atlanta, GA
$43
Editorial/subscriptions:
(404) 955-5656

Stores (monthly)
NRF Enterprises, Inc.
New York, NY
$49
Editorial/subscriptions:
(212) 631-7400

Women's Wear Daily (daily)
Fairchild Publications
New York, NY
$89
Editorial: (212) 630-3500
Subscriptions: (800) 289-0273

VACATIONS AND TRAVEL

Corporate Travel (monthly)
Miller Freeman, Inc.
New York, NY
$65
Editorial/subscriptions:
(212) 869-1300

Mass Transit (bimonthly)
PTN Publishing Company
Melville, NY
$40
Editorial/subscriptions:
(516) 845-2700

Railway Age (monthly)
Simmons-Boardman Publishing Corporation
New York, NY
$45 (controlled circulation)
Editorial: (212) 620-7200
Subscriptions: (800) 228-9670

Travel Weekly (twice weekly)
Reed Travel Group
Secaucus, NJ
$26
Editorial: (201) 902-1500
Subscriptions: (800) 360-0015

SPORTS AND EXERCISE

Sport (monthly)
Peterson Publishing Company
Los Angeles, CA
$17.94
Editorial: (310) 854-2222
Subscriptions (800) 800-8326

Sporting News (weekly)
The Sporting News Publishing Company
St. Louis, MO
$82.80
Editorial: (314) 997-7111
Subscriptions: (800) 777-6785

ELECTRONIC RESOURCES

In addition to libraries, sources of information can be found through computer connections to specialized information vendors and electronic databases. These sources are not free, but they are efficient, powerful resources that include digital collections of information on virtually any subject. Their value lies in the ability of a computerized search to find material by broad or narrow search definitions.

Many libraries are also hooked up to these services and other electronic sources, in addition to rapidly expanding their use of computerized book and periodical catalog collections. These catalogs often have online encyclopedias, almanacs, and other useful reference material. For an introduction to the world of electronic information, check your local library first!

America Online
America Online, Inc.
Vienna, VA
Information databases, news,
conferences, and access to the
Internet
$9.95 per month, $3.50 per hour
with 5 free hours per month
Editorial: (800) 227-6364
Subscriptions: (800) 827-6364

Compuserve
Compuserve, Inc.
Columbus, OH
A few databases, but mostly
devoted to information sharing,
electronic conferences, and access to
the Internet
$40 sign-up fee, $9 per month for
basic services
Editorial: (800) 848-8199
Subscriptions: (800) 554-4079

DIALOG
Dialog Information Services, Inc.
Palo Alto, CA
Information services with more
than 300 databases focusing on
business and technology, and e-mail
service
$295 sign-up fee, rates from $0.25 to
$5.00 per minute
Editorial: (415) 858-3785
Subscriptions: (800) 334-2564

Dow Jones News/Retrieval Service
Dow Jones & Company, Inc.
Princeton, NJ
More than 60 databases with a
focus on finance and business
$1.95 per minute
Editorial: (609) 520-8349
Subscriptions: (800) 522-3567

XPRESS XCHANGE
Denver, CO
A cable-based information system
with a focus on news, education,
and finance
$149.50 one-time purchase of
decoding box, $21.95 monthly fee
for stock quotation service
Subscriptions: (800) 772-6397

STATE RESOURCES

Most individual states issue periodic information about demographic and statistical changes within their boundaries. The following list includes the major publications that are available and information, when available, about publishing schedules. Prices and/or subscription rates can be obtained from the publishing office. Changes in state budgets and political control may alter these publishing programs. To locate a specific title, ask a librarian about interlibrary loans, or contact individual states through departments of commerce or economic research.

Other good sources of state-level demographic data are the Census Bureau-affiliated State Data Centers, which are clearinghouses for census and other data. There is at least one agency in each state that serves this purpose. To get information on any of the State Data Centers, contact the Census Bureau at (301) 763-4683.

Almanac of the 50 States (annual)
Edith Hornor, editor
Information Publications
Palo Alto, CA
(415) 965-4449

The Book of the States (annual)
The Council of State Governments
Lexington, KY
606) 231-1939

ALABAMA

Alabama County Data Book (annual)
Alabama Department of Economic
and Community Affairs,
Planning and Economic
Development Division
Tuscaloosa, AL
(205) 242-5442

Economic Abstract of Alabama
(annual)
University of Alabama, Center for
Business and Economic Research
Tuscaloosa, AL
(205) 348-6191

ALASKA

*The Alaska Economy Performance
Report* (annual)
Alaska Department of Commerce
and Economic Development
Juneau, AK
(907) 465-2017

*Alaska Review of Social and
Economic Conditions* (irregular)
University of Alaska,
Institute of Social and Economic
Research
Anchorage, AK
(907) 786-7710

ARIZONA

Arizona Statistical Abstract (annual)
University of Arizona,
Economic and Business Research,
College of Business and Public
Administration
Tucson, AZ
(602) 621-2155

ARKANSAS

Arkansas Statistical Abstract
(biennial)
University of Arkansas at Little
Rock, State Data Center
Little Rock, AR
(501) 569-8530

CALIFORNIA

California Statistical Almanac
(biennial)
California Department of Finance,
Finance and Economic Research
Unit
Sacramento, CA
(916) 322-2263

COLORADO

Statistical Abstract of Colorado, 1987
University of Colorado, Business
Research Division
Boulder, CO
(303) 492-8227

CONNECTICUT

Connecticut Market Data (biennial)
Connecticut Department of
Economic Development
Rocky Hill, CT
(203) 258-4238

DELAWARE

Delaware Data Book (annual)
Delaware Development Office
Dover, DE
(302) 739-4271

DISTRICT OF COLUMBIA
Indices — A Statistical Index to DC Services (annual)
Office of Policy and Program Evaluation,
Executive Office of the Mayor
Washington, DC
(202) 727-6980

FLORIDA
Florida Statistical Abstract (annual)
University of Florida,
Bureau of Economic and Business Research
Gainesville, FL
(904) 392-0171

GEORGIA
Georgia Statistical Abstract (annual)
University of Georgia,
Terry College of Business,
Selig Center for Economic Growth
Athens, GA
(706) 542-4085

HAWAII
The State of Hawaii Data Book: A Statistical Abstract (annual)
Hawaii State Department of Business,
Economic Development and Tourism Information Office
Honolulu, HI
(808) 586-2355

IDAHO
Idaho Demographic Profile (annual)
Idaho Department of Employment, Research and Analysis Bureau
Boise, ID
(208) 334-6100

Idaho Facts (annual)
Idaho Department of Commerce
Boise, ID
(208) 334-2470

ILLINOIS
Illinois Statistical Abstract (annual)
University of Illinois,
Bureau of Economic and Business Research,
College of Commerce and Business Administration
Champaign, IL
(217) 333-2330

INDIANA
Indiana Factbook (irregular)
Indiana University Business Research Center,
School of Business
Indianapolis, IN
(317) 274-2204

IOWA
Statistical Profile of Iowa (annual)
Iowa Department of Economic Development Research Bureau
Des Moines, IA
(515) 242-4878

KANSAS
Kansas Statistical Abstract (annual)
University of Kansas, Institute for Public Policy and Business Research
Lawrence, KS
(913) 864-3701

KENTUCKY
Kentucky Economic Statistics (annual)
Kentucky Department of Existing Business and Industry
Frankfort, KY
(502) 564-4886

LOUISIANA
Statistical Abstract of Louisiana
(irregular)
University of New Orleans,
Division of Business and Economic
Research
New Orleans, LA
(504) 286-6248

MAINE
Maine: A Statistical Summary
(irregular)
Maine Department of Economic and
Community Development
Augusta, ME
(207) 289-2656

MARYLAND
Maryland Statistical Abstract
(biennial)
Maryland Department of Economic
and Employment Development
Baltimore, MD
(410) 333-6955

MASSACHUSETTS
*Massachusetts Municipal and County
Profiles* (annual)
Information Publications
Palo Alto, CA
(415) 965-4449

MICHIGAN
Michigan Statistical Abstract
(irregular)
Wayne State University
Bureau of Business Research
Detroit, MI
(313) 577-4213

MINNESOTA
*Compare Minnesota: An Economic and
Statistical Factbook* (irregular)
Minnesota Department of Trade
and Economic Development,
Business Development and Analysis
Division
St. Paul, MN
(612) 296-1778

MISSISSIPPI
Mississippi Statistical Abstract
(annual)
Mississippi State University,
College of Business and Industry,
Division of Research
Mississippi State, MS
(601) 325-3817

MISSOURI
Statistical Abstract for Missouri
(biennial)
University of Missouri
Business and Public Administration
Research Center
Columbia, MO
(314) 882-4805

MONTANA
State Data Center
Census & Economic Information
Center,
Montana Department of Commerce
Helena, MT
(406) 444-2896

NEBRASKA
Nebraska Statistical Handbook
(biennial)
Nebraska Department of Economic
Development, Division of Research
Lincoln, NE
(402) 471-3111

NEVADA

Nevada Statistical Abstract (biennial)
Nevada Department of
Administration, Planning Division
Carson City, NV
(702) 687-4065

NEW HAMPSHIRE

State Data Center
Office of State Planning
Concord, NH
(603) 271-2155

NEW JERSEY

New Jersey Statistical Factbook
(annual)
State Data Center
New Jersey Department of Labor
Trenton, NJ
(609) 984-2593

New Jersey Municipal Data Book
(annual)
Information Publications
Palo Alto, CA
(415) 965-4449

NEW MEXICO

New Mexico Statistical Abstract
(irregular)
University of New Mexico,
Bureau of Business and Economic
Research
Albuquerque, NM
(505) 277-2216

NEW YORK

New York State Statistical Yearbook
(annual)
Nelson Rockefeller Institute of
Government
Albany, NY
(518) 443-5522

NORTH CAROLINA

*Statistical Abstract of North Carolina
Counties* (irregular)
Office of State Planning
Raleigh, NC
(919) 733-4131

NORTH DAKOTA

*The Statistical Abstract of North
Dakota, 1988*
University of North Dakota, Bureau
of Business and Economic Research
Grand Forks, ND
(701) 777-3365

OHIO

Benchmark Ohio (biennial)
Ohio State University,
School of Public Policy and
Management
Columbus, OH
(405) 292-8696

OKLAHOMA

Statistical Abstract of Oklahoma
(annual)
University of Oklahoma Center
for Economic and Management
Research
Norman, OK
(405) 325-2931

OREGON

Oregon Blue Book (biennial)
Oregon Secretary of State
Salem, OR
(503) 373-7570

PENNSYLVANIA
Pennsylvania Statistical Abstract (irregular)
State Data Center
Pennsylvania State University, Institute of State and Regional Affairs
Middleton, PA
(717) 948-6336

RHODE ISLAND
Journal-Bulletin Rhode Island Almanac (annual)
Providence Journal Company
Providence, RI
(401) 277-7000

Rhode Island Basic Economic Statistics (annual)
Rhode Island Department of Economic Development
Providence, RI
(401) 277-2601

SOUTH CAROLINA
South Carolina Statistical Abstract (annual)
South Carolina Division of Research and Statistical Services, Budget and Control Board
Columbia, SC
(803) 734-3788

SOUTH DAKOTA
1990 South Dakota Community Abstracts (irregular)
University of South Dakota, State Data Center
Vermillion, SD
(605) 677-5287

TENNESSEE
Tennessee Statistical Abstract (annual)
University of Tennessee Center for Business and Economic Research
Knoxville, TN
(615) 974-5441

TEXAS
Texas Almanac (annual)
Dallas Morning News
Dallas, TX
(214) 977-8261

Texas Fact Book (irregular)
University of Texas Bureau of Business Research
Austin, TX
(512) 471-5180

UTAH
Statistical Abstract of Utah (triennial)
University of Utah Bureau of Economic and Business Research
Salt Lake City, UT
(801) 581-6333

Utah Economic and Demographic Profiles (annual)
Utah Office of Planning and Budget, Demographic and Economic Analysis Section
Salt Lake City, UT
(801) 538-1036

VERMONT
Demographic and Economic Profiles (irregular)
Vermont Office of Policy Research and Coordination, Department of Employment and Training
Montpelier, VT
(802) 229-0311 ext. 323

VIRGINIA

Virginia Statistical Abstract (biennial)
University of Virginia Center for
Public Service
Charlottesville, VA
(804) 982-5551

WASHINGTON

Washington State Data Book
(biennial)
Washington State Office of
Financial Management,
Forecasting Division
Olympia, WA
(206) 753-5617

WEST VIRGINIA

*West Virginia: Economic-Statistical
Profile* (biennial)
West Virginia Chamber of
Commerce
Charleston, WV
(304) 342-1115

WISCONSIN

Wisconsin Blue Book (biennial)
Wisconsin Department of
Administration, Document Sales
Madison, WI
(608) 266-3358

WYOMING

Wyoming Data Handbook (biennial)
Wyoming Department of
Administration and Information,
Economic Analysis Division
Cheyenne, WY
(307) 777-7504

About the Author

Since 1983, Kim Long has researched and written eleven annual editions of *The American Forecaster Almanac.* His ability to track trends on a wide range of subjects makes this work an excellent tool for the business professional. His 80 percent forecast accuracy has extended through the ten previous editions of the book, which the media have widely referred to as they look at upcoming years.

The author's distinctive method of forecasting is accomplished by relying heavily on the traditional skills of journalism—objective analysis of observable phenomena. His predictions are based on comparisons with other consumer product fads, analysis from industry experts, and in-depth investigative reporting.

While there are numerous professional forecasters in various industries, their information is shared only through occasional articles and interviews. Long's ability to take a comprehensive look at the coming year and the accuracy of his forecasts have caused him to be in great demand by the media, businesses, associations, and trade groups throughout the country. For the past five years, national television networks have featured an "end-of-year" story about *The American Forecaster.* From the Associated Press to *CBS This Morning, The American Forecaster* is in regular use as a tool to prepare and present information about the future.

Mr. Long is a 1971 graduate of Wesleyan University. He has been involved with creative projects in the book industry since 1974, writing and producing more than 30 books. His other publications include *The Encyclopedia of Educational Destinations, The Directory of Educational Contests, The Almanac of Anniversaries, The Moon Book,* and *The Astronaut Training Book for Kids.* Mr. Long lives in Denver, Colorado.

Other books from American Demographics

THE INSIDER'S GUIDE TO DEMOGRAPHIC KNOW-HOW: How to Find, Analyze, and Use Information About Your Customers
A comprehensive directory, explaining where to find the data you need, often at little or no cost. Now in its third edition.

**HEALTH CARE CONSUMERS IN THE 1990s:
A Handbook of Trends, Techniques, and Information Sources for Health Care Executives**
This handbook makes the connection between demographic realities and related health care issues. It will help you define your target market and carve out a niche that you can serve profitably and effectively.

**TARGETING FAMILIES:
Marketing To and Through the New Family**
Word-of-mouth product recommendations made from one family member to another are significantly more effective than those made between friends or colleagues. Learn how to get family members on your sales force and how to implement a "Full Family Marketing" approach that attracts youths, spouses, and seniors.

THE BABY BUST: A Generation Comes of Age
As a generation, busters are unique in their experiences, beliefs, politics, and preferences. This is the first statistical biography of this generation. It tells their story through demographics, opinion polls, expert analysis, anecdotes, and the indispensable comments and experiences of busters themselves.

**CAPTURING CUSTOMERS:
How to Target the Hottest Markets of the '90s**
Find out how to use consumer information to identify opportunities in nearly every market niche.

**BEYOND MIND GAMES:
The Marketing Power of Psychographics**
The first book that details what psychographics is, where it came from, and how you can use it.

SELLING THE STORY: The Layman's Guide to
Collecting and Communicating Demographic Information

A handbook offering a crash course in demography and solid instruction in writing about numbers. Learn how to use numbers carefully, how to avoid misusing them, and how to bring cold numbers to life by relating them to real people.

THE SEASONS OF BUSINESS:
The Marketer's Guide to Consumer Behavior

Learn which demographic groups are the principle players and which consumer concerns are most pressing in each marketing season.

DESKTOP MARKETING: Lessons from America's Best

Dozens of case studies show you how top corporations in all types of industries use today's technology to find tomorrow's customers.

Also from American Demographics

AMERICAN DEMOGRAPHICS MAGAZINE is your guide to understanding today's consumer marketplace. It does more than report on the trends; it provides unique insights on your customers and prospects. Annual subscription $62

THE NUMBERS NEWS is a monthly newsletter about the trends defining U.S. consumer markets in the 1990s and beyond. As the population becomes increasingly diverse, you need the most up-to-date information available about demographics and consumer trends. To stay ahead of your competition, you need it first. Annual subscription $149

MARKETING POWER is an all-inclusive catalog of books, topical reprint packages, slides, audio cassettes, speech transcripts, software, and other products for marketing and planning professionals. Request your free copy today!

For more information about
American Demographics publications,
contact our Customer Service Center at
800-828-1133